AAT POCKET NOTES

Technician Level

Unit 11

Drafting Financial Statements

ISBN 1 84390 344 X

British Library Cataloguing-in-Publication data
A catalogue record for this book is available from the British Library.

We are grateful to the Association of Accounting Technicians for permission to reproduce past assessment materials. The solutions have been prepared by FTC Foulks Lynch.

Published by

FTC Foulks Lynch Ltd
Swift House
Market Place
Wokingham
RG40 1AP

Printed and bound in Great Britain

Contents

CHAPTER 1

The regulatory framework

1 The regulatory framework

The regulatory framework for company accounts is based on the following main sources of rules:

- Companies Act 1985
- Accounting standards – SSAPs and FRSs
- Stock exchange regulations (for listed companies).

The standard-setting process in the UK

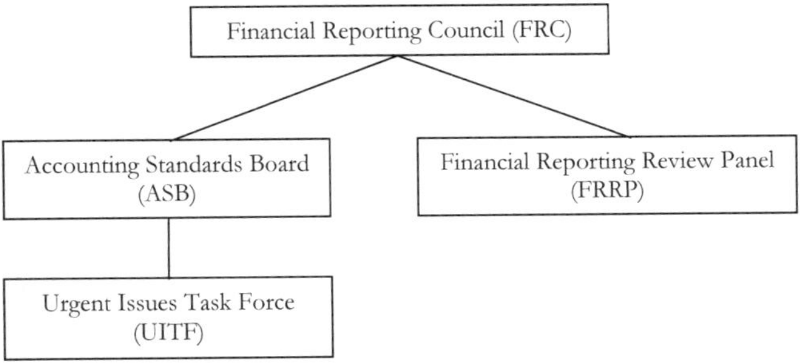

The Financial Reporting Council (FRC)

The FRC supervises the activities of the ASB and the FRRP to ensure that they operate effectively and are adequately funded.

The Accounting Standards Board (ASB)

The role of the ASB is to formulate, issue and revise accounting standards.

A $\frac{2}{3}$ majority is required for any decision to adopt, revise or withdraw an accounting standard.

The Urgent Issues Task Force (UITF)

The UITF reports to the ASB. The role of the UITF is to assist the ASB in areas where an accounting standard or Companies Act provision exists, but where unsatisfactory or conflicting interpretations have developed or seem likely to develop.

The Financial Reporting Review Panel (FRRP)

The FRRP examines apparent departures by public companies and large private companies from the requirements of the Companies Acts and accounting standards in their annual accounts.

The Panel can ask directors to explain such apparent departures, and may ask them to voluntarily withdraw their accounts and replace them with revised accounts that correct the disputed items.

If the company refuses to alter their accounts, the Panel has the right to secure a court order forcing the necessary revision of the accounts.

The International Accounting Standards Committee (IASC)

The IASC has the objective of achieving harmonisation of financial reporting practices worldwide.

The International Accounting Standards Board (IASB), one of the committees within the IASC structure, issues International Accounting Standards (IASs) to further the IASC's objective.

However, in the UK, IASs currently have no direct authority. Companies issuing financial statements in the UK must comply with UK accounting standards (SSAPs and FRSs).

2 Developing an accounting standard

The Foreword to Accounting Standards explains the ASB's process for developing a new FRS.

- ASB identifies a new topic.
- ASB commissions its own staff to conduct research in this area.
- A discussion draft or discussion paper will normally be produced and circulated to those parties who have registered their interest in this topic.
- An exposure draft of an accounting standard (called a Financial Reporting Exposure Draft or FRED) is then published.
- Feedback is received on the FRED - ASB will refine its proposals.
- FRS is issued.

The Foreword states that SSAPs and FRSs must be applied to all accounts intended to give a true and fair view.

CHAPTER 2

The conceptual framework

1 Fundamental accounting concepts

CA85 refers to certain fundamental concepts which must be observed in preparing accounts.

- Going concern
- Prudence
- Consistency
- Matching
- Separate determination or non-aggregation

2 Other accounting concepts

The non-aggregation principle (Companies Act 1985)

In determining items in the accounts, assets and liabilities should not be offset against one another.

The concept of 'true and fair'

The Companies Act 1985 requires that the balance sheet shall give a *true and fair* view of the state of the affairs of the company as at the end of the financial year, and that the profit and loss account shall give a *true and fair* view of the profit or loss of the company for the financial year.

Substance over form

Transactions are accounted for in accordance with their economic substance and financial reality and not merely with their legal form.

For example, leasehold buildings are treated as a fixed asset, provided that it is made clear that the premises are leasehold.

Materiality

An item in a financial statement is material if it is probable that the judgement of a reasonable person relying upon the report would have been changed or influenced by its omission or mis-statement.

Realisation

Revenues and profit can be treated as realised when the receipt of cash or other assets is reasonably certain.

Objectivity

Financial statements should be prepared with the minimum amount of bias.

Historical cost

Quantitative information recorded in monetary values is normally retained at its historical cost.

3 The Statement of Principles

The ASB has published a Statement of Principles, which is intended to lay out the conceptual underpinning of the accounting standards that are issued.

The Statement of Principles is split up into eight chapters, each of which deals with a particular topic.

Chapter 1: The objective of financial statements

The objective is stated as to provide information useful to a wide range of users. Information is required on:

- financial position – balance sheet
- performance – profit and loss account and statement of total recognised gains and losses
- financial adaptability – cash flow statement and certain notes to the accounts

Chapter 2: The reporting entity

An entity should prepare and publish financial statements if there is a legitimate demand for the information, and it is a cohesive economic unit.

Chapter 3: The qualitative characteristics of financial information

Threshold quality: Information is only useful if it is *material* (ie if its omission or mis-statement could influence economic decisions taken by users on the basis of the information).

Subject to the threshold quality of materiality, the chapter identifies four characteristics that make financial information useful to users:

- relevance - can influence decisions
- reliability - a complete and faithful representation
- comparability - for an enterprise over time and between enterprises
- understandability – to a user with a reasonable knowledge of business

Chapter 4: The elements of financial statements

Seven elements of financial statements:

Assets	=	Rights or other access to future economic benefits controlled by an entity as a result of past transactions or events.
Liabilities	=	An entity's obligations to transfer economic benefits as a result of past transactions or events.
Ownership interest	=	The residual amount found by deducting all liabilities of the entity from all of the entity's assets.
Gains	=	Increases in ownership interest other than those relating to contributions from owners.
Losses	=	Decreases in ownership interest other than those relating to distributions to owners.
Contributions from owners	=	Increases in ownership interest resulting from investments made by owners in their capacity as owners.
Distributions to owners	=	Decreases in ownership interest resulting from transfers made to owners in their capacity as owners.

Chapter 5: Recognition in financial statements

An item should be recognised in financial statements if:

- the item meets the definition of an element of financial statements (asset, liability, gain, loss etc), and
- there is sufficient evidence that the *change in assets or liabilities* inherent in the item has occurred (including where appropriate, evidence that a future inflow or outflow of benefit will occur); and
- the item can be *measured* at a monetary amount with sufficient *reliability*.

Chapter 6: Measurement in financial statements

Possible bases are:

- historical cost
- replacement cost
- present value of future cash flows (= economic value = value in use)
- net realisable value

The basis chosen should be the one that best meets the objective of financial statements and the demands of the qualitative characteristics of financial information.

Chapter 7: Presentation of financial information

Primary financial statements:

- the profit and loss account; } statements of financial performance
- the statement of total recognised gains and losses; } statements of financial performance
- the balance sheet; and
- the cash flow statement.

A set of financial statements comprises the primary statements plus supporting notes.

Chapter 8: Accounting for interests in other entities

In the group accounts, the appropriate method of accounting depends on the degree of influence that the parent company exercises over the investee company:

- if the parent controls the investee, the investee's results should be consolidated into the group accounts.
- if the parent has joint control over, or can significantly influence, the investee, then the parent's share of the investee's results should be included in the group accounts.
- if the parent cannot significantly influence the investee, then the investee should be included in the group accounts like any other small investment (ie the same as in the individual accounts stage).

4 FRS 18: Accounting policies

SSAP 2 has been withdrawn and replaced by FRS 18 which is consistent with the Statement of Principles.

The SSAP 2 concepts (going concern, consistency, accruals and prudence) must still be applied when preparing accounts, since the CA 1985 specifically requires their application.

Accounting policies must be selected to enable the financial statements to give a true and fair view.

FRS 18 identifies the going concern concept and the accruals concept as playing a pervasive role in the process of selecting accounting policies:

- an entity should prepare its financial statements on a going concern basis, unless the entity is being liquidated or the directors have no realistic alternative but to cease trading. In such circumstances the financial statements should not apply the going concern basis.
- an entity should prepare its balance sheet and profit and loss account on an accruals basis rather than a strict cash basis.

When choosing accounting policies, an entity should judge possible policies against the objectives of relevance, reliability, comparability and understandability.

Accounting policies should be reviewed regularly to ensure that they remain the most appropriate to the particular circumstances.

Changes in accounting policies should be accounted for as a prior period adjustment in accordance with FRS 3.

Changes in accounting estimates (as opposed to changes in accounting policies) should be reflected in the current (and future) year's results.

Disclosures

Description of all the accounting policies used for material items in the financial statements.

Where a change in accounting policy has been made the entity should disclose the particulars of the change and the reasons why it is believed that the new policy is more appropriate.

The directors should disclose any uncertainties which cast doubt on whether the entity is a going concern.

Where the statutory true and fair view override has been invoked, the entity should disclose the particulars of the matter, the reasons and the effect.

CHAPTER 3

Drafting financial statements

1 Types of profit making organisation

Sole trader

- An organisation owned by one person.
- Accounting conventions recognise the business as a *separate entity* from its owner.
- Legally, the business and personal affairs of a sole trader are not distinguished in any way.
- A sole trader has complete personal unlimited liability.

Partnership

- Two or more persons associated for the purpose of a business or a profession.
- A partnership is not legally distinguished from its members. Personal assets of the partners may have to be used to pay the debts of the partnership business.

The advantages of trading as a partnership:

- More resources may be available, including capital, specialist knowledge, skills and ideas.
- Administrative expenses may be lower for a partnership than for the equivalent number of sole traders, due to economies of scale.
- Partners can substitute for each other.

Limited company

- A distinct, artificial 'person' created in order to separate legal responsibility for the affairs of a business (or any other activity) from the personal affairs of the individuals who own and/or operate the business.
- The owners are known as *shareholders* (or members) and the people who run the business are known as *directors*. In a small corporation, owners and directors are often the same people.

Limited liability

Limited liability refers to the liability of each shareholder being limited to any unpaid amount on their shares.

Comparison of limited companies to sole traders and partnerships

The fact that a company is a separate legal entity means that it is very different from a sole trader or partnership in a number of ways.

- The property of a registered company belongs to the company. A change in the ownership of shares in the company will have no effect on the ownership of the company's property.
- Shares in a registered company can usually be transferred without the consent of the other shareholders. In a partnership, in the absence of agreement to the contrary, a new partner cannot be introduced into a firm without the consent of all existing partners.
- A registered company can contract with its members and can sue and be sued on such contracts. A partner cannot enter into contracts with his own firm, nor can a sole trader.
- As a separate legal person, a company can sue and be sued in its own name. Judgements relating to companies do not affect the members personally.
- There is no upper limit on the number of members in a company. In a partnership, except in certain restricted categories, such as accountants and stockbrokers, the maximum number of partners is 20.
- A company has greater scope for raising loans by, for example, borrowing on debentures and may secure them with floating charges.
- A company is legally separate from its members and is taxed separately from its members.

Disadvantages of incorporation

- When they are being formed, companies have to register and to file a Memorandum and Articles of Association (formal constitution documents) with the Registrar. Registration fees and legal costs have to be paid.
- The accounts of larger limited companies are subject to an annual audit inspection (this requirement has been lifted for small companies).
- A registered company's accounts and certain other documents are open to public inspection. The accounts of sole traders and partnerships are not open to public inspection.
- Limited companies are subject to strict rules in connection with the introduction and withdrawal of capital and profits.
- Members of a company may not take part in its management unless they are directors, whereas all partners are entitled to share in management, unless the partnership agreement provides otherwise.

2 Types of non-profit making entities

The main types of non–profit making entity are:

- clubs and societies
- charities
- public sector organisations (including central government, local government and National Health Service bodies).

Objectives of profit making and 'not for profit' entities compared

- The main objective of sole traders, partnerships and limited companies is normally assumed as being to make a profit.
- The main objective of charities, clubs and societies is to carry out the activities for which they were created.
- The main objective of public sector organisations is to provide services to the general public.

Other differences between profit making and non-profit making entities

	Profit making	**Clubs, societies, charities**	**Public sector**
Managed by:	Sole traders, partners, directors (who may also be shareholders)	Depends on constitution/other internal regulations	Elected officials, eg MPs, councillors
Main sources of finance:	Personal capacity, equity, debt	Donations, membership fees	Taxation
Stewardship responsibilities to: (likely to be main users of financial statements)	Shareholders	Members, donors, beneficiaries	The general public

	Profit making	Clubs, societies, charities	Public sector
Financial statements used to assess:	Financial performance, whether to hold or sell investment	Whether resources have been used efficiently to achieve objectives	Level of spending in relation to services provided, whether services provide value for money, whether services have been provided economically efficiently, effectively

Accounts of non-profit making entities

Most non–profit making entities prepare a statement of financial performance (the equivalent of a profit and loss account for a profit making entity) and a balance sheet. Many entities also prepare a cash flow statement.

3 Preparing final accounts

Final accounts are the end result of a process of summarising, classifying and structuring large quantities of data. The objective of preparing final accounts is to turn individual transactions into useful information.

The profit and loss account of a sole trader

The *profit and loss account* is a summary of a business's transactions for a given period. In practice, as you will see from the following pro forma, it is commonly split into two parts and referred to as a *trading and profit and loss account.*

Proforma trading and profit and loss account for the year ended ...

			£	£
①	**Sales**			X
	Less:	**Cost of sales**		
		Stock, at cost on 1 January (opening stock)	X	
		Add: Purchases of goods	X	
			X	
	Less:	Stock, at cost on 31 December (closing stock)	(X)	
				(X)
②	**Gross profit**			X
	Sundry income:			
		Discounts received	X	
		Commission received	X	
		Rent received	X	
				X
				X
	Less:	Other expenses:		
		Rent	X	
		Rates	X	
		Lighting and heating	X	
		Telephone	X	
		Postage	X	
		Insurance	X	
		Stationery	X	
		Office salaries	X	
		Depreciation	X	
		Accountancy and audit fees	X	
		Bank charges and interest	X	
		Bad and doubtful debts	X	
		Delivery costs	X	
		Van running expenses	X	
		Advertising	X	
		Discounts allowed	X	
				(X)
	Net profit			X

① – **Trading account**

② – **Profit and loss account**

The balance sheet of a sole trader

The *balance sheet* is a statement of the financial position of a business at a given date, usually the end of the period covered by the *profit and loss account*. It is a snapshot at one given moment.

Pro forma balance sheet at ......

	Cost	*Depreciation*	
	£	£	£
Fixed assets			
Freehold factory	X	X	X
Machinery	X	X	X
Motor vehicles	X	X	X
	X	X	X
Current assets			
Stocks		X	
Debtors	X		
Less: Prov for doubtful debts	(X)	X	
Prepayments		X	
Cash at bank		X	
Cash in hand		X	
		X	
Current liabilities			
Trade creditors	X		
Accrued charges	X		
		(X)	
Net current assets			X
			X
Long-term liabilities			
12% loan			(X)
Net assets			X
Representing:			
Capital at 1 January			X
Profit for the year			X
			X
Less: Drawings			(X)
Proprietor's funds			X

4 *Making adjustments*

Adjustments to the initial trial balance, the extended trial balance and the draft accounts are made by drawing up and posting a *journal entry*.

Journals

In practice, journals may be used in several ways:

- to record major or unusual transactions
- to record period-end adjustments (eg depreciation, stock, doubtful debts)
- to facilitate the correction of errors, and to explain the nature of the errors

Journals are recorded in the journal book. This is a book of prime entry and is not part of the double entry. From the journal book, the journals are posted to the relevant accounts in the nominal ledger.

5 *The extended trial balance*

A **trial balance** is simply a list of all the balances on the ledger accounts *before* year-end adjustments are made. These adjustments need to be made before the preparation of the profit and loss account and balance sheet and they normally include the following:

- correction of errors
- recognition of accruals and prepayments
- provision of the year's depreciation charge
- review of the charge for bad and doubtful debts
- inclusion of closing stock

The **extended trial balance** is a worksheet which takes us from the trial balance to the profit and loss account and balance sheet.

Layout of a typical extended trial balance

Account	*Trial balance*		*Adjustments*		*Profit and loss account*		*Balance sheet*	
	Dr £	*Cr* £	*Dr* £	*Cr* £	*Dr* £	*Cr* £	*Dr* £	*Cr* £

Example

Trial balance at 31 December 20X6

	Dr	Cr
	£	£
Shop fittings at cost	2,000	
Depreciation provision at 1 January 20X6		100
Leasehold premises at cost	12,500	
Depreciation provision at 1 January 20X6		625
Stock in trade at 1 January 20X6	26,000	
Debtors at 31 December 20X6	53,000	
Provision for doubtful debts at 1 January 20X6		960
Cash in hand	50	
Cash at bank	2,250	
Creditors for supplies		65,000
Proprietor's capital at 1 January 20X6		28,115
Drawings to 31 December 20X6	2,000	
Purchases	102,000	
Sales		129,000
Wages	18,200	
Advertising	2,300	
Rates for 15 months to 31 March 20X7	1,500	
Light and heat	1,800	
Bank charges	200	
	223,800	223,800

The following adjustments are to be made:

(1) Depreciation of shop fittings £100
Depreciation of leasehold premises £625

(2) A debt of £500 is irrecoverable and is to be written off; the doubtful debts provision is to be increased to 2% of the debtors.

(3) Advertising fees of £200 have been treated incorrectly as wages.

(4) The proprietor has withdrawn goods costing £1,000 for his personal use; these have not been recorded as drawings.

(5) The stock in trade at 31 December 20X6 is valued at £30,000.

(6) The electricity charge for the last three months of 20X6 is outstanding and is estimated to be £400.

Prepare the extended trial balance at 31 December 20X6.

Solution

Step 1: The balances per the trial balance are recorded in the correct columns and the total of the debit balances is agreed to the total of the credit balances.

Step 2: We shall now deal with the adjustments (apart from accruals and prepayments).

- **Correction of errors**

(i) Drawings of the proprietor:

		£	£
Debit	Drawings	1,000	
Credit	Purchases		1,000

(ii) Mis-classification of advertising fees as wages:

Debit	Advertising	200	
Credit	Wages		200

- **Provision of the year's depreciation charge**

Debit	Depreciation expense: shop fittings	100	
Debit	Depreciation expense: leasehold premises	625	
Credit	Provision for depreciation: shop fittings		100
Credit	Provision for depreciation: leasehold premises		625

We will need to set up the depreciation expense account as none exists.

- **Provision for doubtful debts**

Debit	Bad and doubtful debts expense	590	
Credit	Provision for doubtful debts (1,050 – 960)		90
Credit	Debtors		500

The bad debt expense account will need to be created.

- **Inclusion of closing stock**

Debit	Stock (balance sheet)	30,000	
Credit	Stock (profit and loss account)		30,000

Step 3: We now have to deal with the last adjustments, ie the accruals and prepayments.

- **Electricity**

Debit	Light and heat	400	
Credit	Accruals		400

The accruals account will need to be set up.

- **Rates**

Debit	Prepayments (1,500 × $\frac{3}{15}$)	300	
Credit	Rates		300

The prepayments account will need to be set up.

Step 4: We have now recorded all of the adjustments and we need to prepare the trading and profit and loss account and balance sheet columns. This is achieved by extending each account balance across to the appropriate profit and loss or balance sheet columns.

Step 5: The trading and profit and loss account and balance sheet are then prepared from the relevant columns.

The completed extended trial balance is shown below:

Extended trial balance at 31 December 20X6

Account	*Trial balance*		*Adjustments*		*Profit and loss account*		*Balance sheet*	
	Dr	*Cr*	*Dr*	*Cr*	*Dr*	*Cr*	*Dr*	*Cr*
	£	£	£	£	£	£	£	£
Shop fittings	2,000						2,000	
Provision for depreciation 1.1.X6		100		100				200
Leasehold premises	12,500						12,500	
Provision for depreciation 1.1.X6		625		625				1,250
Stock 1.1.X6	26,000		30,000	30,000	26,000	30,000	30,000	
Debtors	53,000			500			52,500	
Provision for doubtful debts 1.1.X6		960		90				1,050
Cash in hand	50						50	
Cash at bank	2,250						2,250	
Creditors		65,000						65,000
Capital		28,115						28,115
Drawings	2,000		1,000				3,000	
Purchases	102,000			1,000	101,000			
Sales		129,000				129,000		
Wages	18,200			200	18,000			
Advertising	2,300		200		2,500			
Rates	1,500			300	1,200			
Light and heat	1,800		400		2,200			
Bank charges	200				200			
Depreciation – shop fittings			100		100			
Depreciation – leasehold premises			625		625			
Bad debts expense			590		590			
Prepayments			300				300	
Accruals				400				400
					152,415	159,000		
Net profit					6,585			6,585
	223,800	223,800	33,215	33,215	159,000	159,000	102,600	102,600

The trading and profit and loss account and balance sheet are now drafted from the extended trial balance.

Trading and profit and loss account for the year ended 31 December 20X6

		£	£
Sales			129,000
Less:	Cost of sales		
	Opening stock	26,000	
	Purchases	101,000	
		127,000	
	Closing stock	(30,000)	
			(97,000)
Gross profit			32,000
Less:	Expenses		
	Wages	18,000	
	Advertising	2,500	
	Rates	1,200	
	Light and heat	2,200	
	Bank charges	200	
	Depreciation (100 + 625)	725	
	Bad debts	590	
			(25,415)
Net profit			6,585

Balance sheet at 31 December 20X6

	Cost	Accumulated depreciation	Net book value
	£	£	£
Fixed assets			
Shop fittings	2,000	200	1,800
Leasehold premises	12,500	1,250	11,250
	14,500	1,450	13,050
Current assets			
Stocks		30,000	
Debtors (52,500 – 1,050)		51,450	
Prepayments		300	
Cash at bank		2,250	
Cash in hand		50	
		84,050	
Current liabilities			
Creditors	65,000		
Accruals	400		
		(65,400)	
Net current assets			18,650
			31,700
Represented by:			
Capital			28,115
Add: Net profit for the year			6,585
			34,700
Less: Drawings			(3,000)
			31,700

6 From trial balance to final accounts

In an assessment it is more likely that you will be required to prepare a set of final accounts from a trial balance and a given set of adjustments to the trial balance figures.

Example

Set out below is the trial balance of Lyttleton, a sole trader, extracted at 31 December 20X5.

	Dr	*Cr*
	£	£
Capital account		7,830
Cash at bank	2,010	
Fixed assets at cost	9,420	
Provision for depreciation at 31 December 20X4		3,470
Debtors	1,830	
Stock at 31 December 20X4	1,680	
Creditors		390
Sales		14,420
Purchases	8,180	
Rent	1,100	
Electricity	940	
Rates	950	
	26,110	26,110

On examination of the accounts, the following information is obtained.

1. Depreciation for the year of £942 is to be charged.
2. A provision for doubtful debts of 3% of total debts is to be set up.
3. Purchases include £1,500 of goods which were bought for the proprietor's personal use.
4. Stock at 31 December 20X5 was £1,140.
5. The rent account shows the monthly payments of £100 made from 1 January to 1 November 20X5 inclusive. Owing to an oversight the payment on 1 December 20X5 was not made.
6. The rates account shows the prepayment of £150 brought forward at the beginning of 20X5 (and representing rates from 1 January 20X5 to 31 March 20X5) together with the £800 payment made on 1 April 20X5 and relating to the period from 1 April 20X5 to 31 March 20X6.
7. The electricity charge for the last three months of 20X5 is outstanding and is estimated to be £400.

Required

Prepare a trading and profit and loss account for the year ended 31 December 20X5 and a balance sheet as at that date.

Solution

Start with the profit and loss account. It is essential that you know the proforma off by heart.

Sales will always be the first figure. Pull it from the trial balance, put it in your trading account and tick the figure on your question to show you've used it.

Repeat this to complete the trading account.

Remember that closing stock will come from your additional information and opening stock from the trial balance.

Also figures in the trial balance are affected by subsequent information as in note 3. Purchases in the trial balance include goods used by the proprietor – drawings. Use a bracket to show your adjustment.

Next deal with expenses.

Put a ruler on the first line of the trial balance. Is the balance an expense?

If no - move down a line.

If yes - refer to the additional information for adjustments, accruals and prepayments and include the total in the profit and loss account. Tick off and move down a line.

Now go through the additional information for further expenses – in this case depreciation and bad debts expense.

Your final trading and profit and loss account should look like this:

Lyttleton trading and profit and loss account for year ended 31 December 20X5

	£	£
Sales		14,420
Cost of sales		
Opening stock	1,680	
Purchases (8,180 – 1,500)	6,680	
	8,360	
Less: Closing stock	(1,140)	
		(7,220)
Gross profit		7,200
Less: Expenses		
Rent (1,100 + 100)	1,200	
Electricity (940 + 400)	1,340	
Rates (950 - ¼ × 800)	750	
Depreciation	942	
Bad and doubtful debts (3% × 1,830)	55	
		(4,287)
Net profit		2,913

Now move on to the balance sheet.

The only balances not ticked should be balance sheet accounts.

Start at the top of the balance sheet with fixed assets and follow the proforma down pulling information from the question as you need it.

Lyttleton balance sheet as at 31 December 20X5

	Cost	*Depn*	
	£	£	£
Fixed assets	9,420	4,412	5,008
Current assets			
Stocks		1,140	
Debtors	1,830		
Provision for doubtful debts	(55)		
		1,775	
Prepayments		200	
Cash		2,010	
		5,125	
Current liabilities			
Creditors	390		
Accruals (100 + 400)	500		
		(890)	
Net current assets			4,235
			9,243
Capital as at 1.1.X5			7,830
Profit for the year			2,913
			10,743
Less: Drawings			(1,500)
			9,243

CHAPTER 4

Preparing limited company accounts

1 Distinctive features of limited companies

A limited company is a separate legal entity and is distinct from its owners. This is in contrast to a sole trader who in law is *not* a separate entity from his business.

Types of limited company

There are two types of limited company, public (Plc) and private (Ltd). The main difference is that a private company may not offer its shares to the public and so all companies listed on the Stock Exchange are public companies.

Advantages of incorporated status

- Limited liability of owners.
- The shareholders can share in the profits of the business without having to work day-to-day for the business.
- Companies are in a better position when borrowing money.
- The company will continue in existence even if shareholders die.

Disadvantages of incorporated status

- A large company must have an audit of its accounts and therefore must pay auditors' fees.
- A large company must publish its accounts on public record.
- A company suffers a greater administration burden than a sole trader.

Distinctions between the accounts of a limited company and a sole trader

- The way in which profit is appropriated in the profit and loss account.
- The composition of capital in the balance sheet.
- The statutory requirements: whereas a sole trader can present their accounts using any format they wish, companies are required by the CA 85 to use specified formats for their published accounts. Of course they can use any format they wish for the accounts that they prepare for internal use (such as monthly management accounts).

Proforma accounts

Proforma profit and loss account for a limited company (for internal use)

		£	£
Sales			X
Opening stock		X	
Add Purchases of goods/transfers from factory		X	
		X	
Less Closing stock		(X)	
Cost of sales			(X)
Gross profit			X
Sundry income			X
			X
Expenses (classified/listed as appropriate)			(X)
Operating profit			X
Interest payable			(X)
Profit before taxation			X
Taxation			(X)
Profit after taxation			X
Dividends	Paid	(X)	
	Proposed	(X)	
			(X)
Retained profit for the financial year			X
Retained profit brought forward			X
Retained profit carried forward			X

Proforma balance sheet for a limited company (for internal use)

	Cost	*Dep'n*	
	£	£	£
Fixed assets			
Freehold factory	X	X	X
Machinery	X	X	X
Motor vehicles	X	X	X
	X	X	X
Current assets			
Stocks		X	
Debtors	X		
Less Provision for doubtful debts	(X)		
		X	
Prepayments		X	
Cash at bank and in hand		X	
		X	
Current liabilities			
Trade creditors	X		
PAYE, NIC and VAT	X		
Corporation tax	X		
Proposed dividends	X		
Accruals	X		
		(X)	
Net current assets			X
Total assets less current liabilities			X
Long-term liabilities			
Debenture loans			(X)
			X
Capital and reserves			
Share capital			X
Share premium account			X
Other reserves			X
Profit and loss account			X
			X

2 The profit and loss account

Corporation tax

The figure for corporation tax is a provision for tax based on the profits for the year. It does not represent the tax paid because corporation tax is not payable immediately but usually nine months after the year end.

The accounting entries are as follows.

Debit Profit and loss account
Credit Corporation tax (shown as a current liability in the balance sheet)

Dividends

Interim dividends

Debit Dividend account (written off to P&L a/c)
Credit Cash

Year end provision for final dividend

Debit Profit and loss account
Credit Dividends proposed account (shown as current liability)

Hence we will have two debits for dividends in the profit and loss account – one paid and one proposed.

3 The balance sheet

The major difference in the balance sheet of a company lies in the capital section, reflecting the differences in the nature of ownership of a company as compared with an unincorporated business.

Debentures

A debenture is a written acknowledgement of a debt by a company. The debt referred to will be the borrowing of money usually for a number of years. This loan will normally carry a fixed rate of interest and may be secured against assets owned by the company.

Share capital and share premium

The ownership of a company is through shares, which have been issued by the company. The bookkeeping entries will be as follows.

Debit Cash
Credit Share capital account

A company may issue different types (classes) of shares.

- *Ordinary shares.* Ordinary shareholders are effectively the owners of the company.
- *Preference shares.* Preference in this context means that the owners of these shares will have priority over the ordinary shareholders in the payment of their dividend, which is usually of a fixed amount.

There are various accounting terms to describe share capital: issued, authorised, called up and paid up.

When a company is first established it must prepare a Memorandum of Association which will state the amount of shares which the company is allowed to issue to its shareholders. This is the *authorised share capital* of the company. There is nothing to compel the company to issue to shareholders all of the shares which it is authorised to issue. The number of shares actually issued is known as the *issued share capital*.

Once the company has asked its shareholders to pay for the shares it has issued to them, the shares are said to be *called up*. Once those shareholders have paid the company for the shares they are said to be *paid up*.

Bonus issues

Sometimes, extra shares may be issued to existing shareholders without any more money having to be paid for them:

Debit Reserves

Credit Ordinary share capital

with the nominal value of the bonus shares issued.

Rights issues

A rights issue differs from a bonus issue in that the company actually raises cash through an additional issue of shares at a favourable price to the existing shareholders. The number of shares that they are entitled to take up will be in proportion to their existing holdings; for example, a one for five rights issue.

Example

XYZ plc has 2,000,000 25p ordinary shares in issue and its summarised balance sheet is given below.

	£000
Net assets	2,300
Capital and reserves	
Share capital (2,000,000 × 25p)	500
Reserves	1,800
	2,300

The company decides to make a rights issue of one for five at £1 each.

Required

Show the balance sheet after the rights issue is complete.

Solution

The rights issue will be 400,000 shares at £1 each and will raise cash of £400,000 which can be split between nominal value and premium as follows.

	£
Nominal value 400,000 × 25p	100,000
Share premium (75p each)	300,000
Cash	400,000

The new balance sheet will be as follows.

	£000
Net assets (2,300 + 400)	2,700
Capital and reserves	
Share capital (500 + 100)	600
Share premium	300
Reserves	1,800
	2,700

Shareholders' options

A shareholder who receives a rights offer has three options open to him.

(a) Take up the rights and pay the required amount to the company, increasing his shareholding.

(b) Sell his rights to a third party who may then buy the shares from the company.

(c) Do nothing and let his rights lapse.

Reserves

These comprise the cumulative total of the company's retained profits. In respect of each accounting period the double entry will be as follows.

Debit Profit and loss account
Credit Reserves account

Appropriation of profits in a limited company

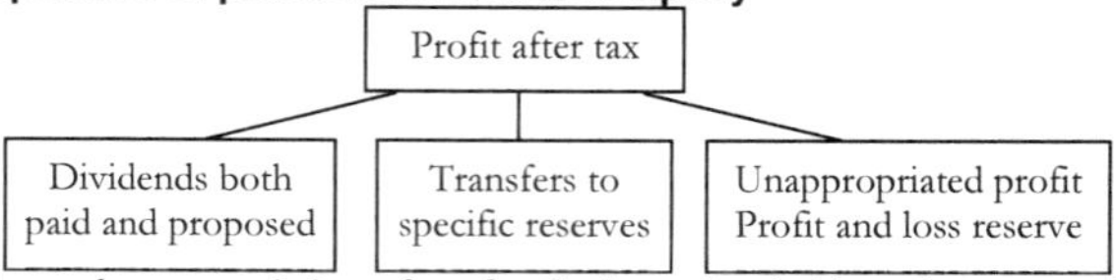

This shows the appropriation of profits firstly to shareholders, then to specific named reserves and then finally the retained profits which go to the profit and loss reserve.

CHAPTER 5

Statutory formats

1 The balance sheet

Format 1

Note	£	£
Fixed assets		
Intangible assets		X
Tangible assets		X
Investments		X
		X
Current assets		
Stocks	X	
Debtors	X	
Investments	X	
Cash at bank and in hand	X	
	X	
Creditors: amounts falling due within one year	(X)	
Net current assets		X
Total assets less current liabilities		X
Creditors: amounts falling due after more than one year		(X)
Provisions for liabilities and charges		(X)
Accruals and deferred income		(X)
		X
Capital and reserves		
Called up share capital		X
Share premium account		X
Revaluation reserve		X
Other reserves (if any)		X
Profit and loss account		X
		X

.... Director

The accounts were approved by the board of directors on ....

2 Notes to the balance sheet

Fixed assets (intangible, tangible and investments): cost or valuation

- Opening balance
- Movements (additions, disposals, revaluations, transfers)
- Closing balance

Depreciation

- Opening balance
- Movements (disposals, charge for year, transfers, revaluations)
- Closing balance

Land and buildings

- Freeholds
- Long leaseholds (at least 50 years to run)
- Short leaseholds (less than 50 years to run)

In relation to fixed assets at valuation (except listed investments), disclose the following.

- Years and amounts of valuation
- If valued during the year, the name or qualification of the valuers and the basis of valuation
- Comparable historical cost (HC) amounts or differences between HC and carrying amounts

Intangible fixed assets

Capitalised development costs – disclose:

- reasons for capitalisation
- write-off period.

Acquired goodwill – disclose:

- write-off period
- reason for period chosen.

Investments

In relation to *all types of investments*, disclose:

- amounts written off
- amounts written back
- fixed asset details, if the investments rank as fixed assets (some investments rank as current assets).

In relation to *listed investments* only, disclose:

- market value, if this is different from book value
- stock exchange value, if this is less than market value
- the amount of tax that would be payable if the investments were sold at valuation.

Illustration

Intangible assets

	Goodwill	*Licences*	*Total*
	£000	*£000*	*£000*
Cost			
At 1 April 20X5 and 31 March 20X6	X	X	X
Amortisation			
At 1 April 20X5	(X)	(X)	(X)
Provision for year	(X)	(X)	(X)
At 31 March 20X6	(X)	(X)	(X)
Net book amount			
At 1 April 20X5	X	X	X
At 31 March 20X6	X	X	X

Tangible assets

	Land and buildings				
		Long	*Short*	*Plant and*	
	Freehold	*Lease*	*Lease*	*Machinery*	*Total*
	£000	*£000*	*£000*	*£000*	*£000*
Cost or valuation					
At 1 April 20X5	X	X	X	X	X
Revaluation	X	–	–	–	X
Additions	X	X	X	X	X
Disposals	(X)	(X)	(X)	(X)	(X)
At 31 March 20X6	X	X	X	X	X

Depreciation					
At 1 April 20X5	X	X	X	X	X
Disposals	(X)	(X)	(X)	(X)	(X)
Provision for year	X	X	X	X	X
At 31 March 20X6	X	X	X	X	X
Net book amount					
At 1 April 20X5	X	X	X	X	X
At 31 March 20X6	X	X	X	X	X

A freehold site was revalued during the year by Messrs Tottitup Chartered Surveyors, on the basis of its current use as a parking lot. If the site were sold for its revalued amount, it is estimated that tax of £X would be payable on the gain.

The historical cost of the site was £Z and it was revalued to £Y. No provision for depreciation has been made.

Stocks

Separate disclosure is required of raw materials, work in progress and finished goods. Disclose also the difference between carrying value and replacement costs for each category, if material.

Debtors

The main categories to be disclosed separately are: trade debtors, other debtors, amounts recoverable on contracts, and prepayments and accrued income. Distinguish between debts falling due within one year of the balance sheet date and debts due more than one year after the balance sheet date.

Creditors

The main categories are shown in the illustration below. Creditors falling due within one year are shown separately from those falling due after more than one year.

Show the following details in relation to secured creditors.

- Type
- Amount
- Nature of security

In relation to debts not wholly payable within five years, disclose:

- the amount payable by instalment
- the amount payable otherwise than by instalment
- the repayment terms
- the rates of interest.

In relation to debentures issued in the year, state:

- the classes issued
- the amount issued and the consideration received by class.

Debentures which are convertible should be disclosed.

Illustration

Creditors: amounts falling due within one year

	£000
Debenture loans	X
Bank loans and overdrafts	X
Payments on account	X
Trade creditors	X
Bills of exchange payable	X
Amounts due to group undertakings	X
Amounts due to undertakings in which the company has a participating interest	X
Other creditors including taxation and social security	
Obligations under finance leases and hire purchase contracts	X
Corporation tax	X
Social security and other taxes	X
Other creditors	X
Accruals and deferred income	X
	X

Loans not wholly repayable within five years

	£000
Repayable by instalments	X
Repayable otherwise	X
	X

Details of loans not wholly repayable within five years are as follows.

	£000
X% debentures repayable in annual instalments of £X commencing 31 Dec 20XX	X
X% secured loan repayable in annual instalments of £X commencing 31 Dec 20XX	X
X% secured US dollar loan repayable on 31 May 20XX	X
	X

The long-term bank loans are secured by fixed charges over various of the group's properties. Bank loans wholly repayable within five years include £X secured by a floating charge over the company's assets.

Provisions for liabilities and charges

Disclose the deferred tax balance and any other provisions.

Called up share capital

Disclose the amount of *authorised* share capital.

For each class of *allotted* share capital, disclose:

- number of shares
- total nominal value.

In relation to redeemable shares, disclose:

- earliest and latest redemption dates
- whether at shareholder's or company option
- premium payable on redemption.

In relation to shares allotted during the year, disclose:

- the classes of shares allotted
- for each class, the number of shares, their nominal value and the consideration received.

In relation to share options, disclose:

- the number, description and amount of shares
- the period of option
- the price.

3 The profit and loss account

Companies Act Format 1 (with additional FRS 3 disclosure) is set out below.

Notes		*Continuing operations*	*Acquisitions*	*Discontinued operations*	*Total*
		£	£	£	£
	Turnover	X	X	X	X
	Cost of sales	(X)	(X)	(X)	(X)
	Gross profit	X	X	X	X
	Distribution costs	(X)	(X)	(X)	(X)
	Administrative expenses	(X)	(X)	(X)	(X)
	Other operating income	X	X	X	X
	Operating profit	X	X	X	X
	Profit on sale of fixed assets	X	X	X	X
	Loss on disposal of discontinued operations			(X)	(X)
	Profit on ordinary activities before interest	X	X	X	X
	Income from shares in group undertakings (not group accounts)				X
	Income from participating interests				X
	Income from other fixed asset investments				X
	Other interest receivable and similar income				X
	Profit on ordinary activities before taxation				X
	Tax on profit on ordinary activities				(X)
	Profit on ordinary activities after taxation				X
	Minority interests				(X)
				£	£
Profit for the financial year					X
Dividends					
	Preference dividend			X	
	Ordinary dividend			X	
					(X)
Retained profit for the financial year					X
Earnings per share (FRS 14 – listed companies)					X

A statement of reserves is provided in Note X.

Although format 1 of the statutory profit and loss account is more commonly seen in practice, some companies choose to present their profit and loss account using format 2.

The top section of a format 2 profit and loss account is set out below

Notes	*Continuing operations*	*Acquisitions*	*Discontinued operations*	*Total*
	£	£	£	£
Turnover	X	X	X	X
Change in stocks of finished goods and work in progress	X	X	X	X
Own work capitalised	X	X	X	X
Other operating income	X	X	X	X
Raw materials and consumables	(X)	(X)	(X)	(X)
Other external charges	(X)	(X)	(X)	(X)
Staff costs *	(X)	(X)	(X)	(X)
Depreciation and other amounts written off tangible and intangible fixed assets	(X)	(X)	(X)	(X)
Operating profit	X	X	X	X
Profit on sale of fixed assets	X	X	X	X
Loss on disposal of discontinued operations	–	–	(X)	(X)
Profit on ordinary activities before interest	X	X	X	X

* may show analysis on face of profit and loss account

A statement of total recognised gains and losses is required by FRS 3, as is a note of historical cost profits and losses.

Some items must be disclosed on the face of the profit and loss account.

- Profit or loss on ordinary activities before taxation.
- Transfers to reserves.
- Dividends paid and proposed (aggregate amount).
- Earnings per share (listed companies only).

Certain disclosures required by FRS 3 must also be shown on the face of the profit and loss account.

- Analysis of turnover and operating profit.
- Profit or loss on sale or termination of operations.
- Costs of a fundamental reorganisation.
- Profit or loss on fixed asset disposal.

4 Notes to the profit and loss account

Accounting policies

- Accounting policies for all material areas, eg depreciation, leased assets, stock valuation.
- Turnover – disclosed by class of business and by geographical market.

Operating costs and revenues

Income: disclose any exceptional income (plus description).

Expenditure: disclose the following.

- Depreciation.
- Auditors' remuneration.
- Exceptional charges (plus description).

Employees

- Average number of employees in year.
- Average number in each category.
- Total wages and salaries.
- Social security costs.
- Other pension costs.

Directors

Disclose the aggregate of emoluments*.

- Include salary, fees, bonuses, benefits in kind.
- Exclude share options, pensions, long-term incentive schemes.

Disclose:

- Gains on exercise of share options (listed companies only).
- Assets (excluding share options and, for non-listed companies, shares) receivable under long-term incentive schemes*.
- Pension contributions paid by the company.

Disclose the number of directors covered by each of two types of pension schemes.

- Money purchase schemes.
- Defined benefit schemes.

For non-listed companies only, disclose the number of directors who:

- exercised share options
- received or became entitled to shares under a long-term incentive scheme.

Where the items marked * total more than £200,000 the following additional disclosures are required in relation to the highest paid director.

- How much of the above amounts are attributable to him/her.
- If covered by a defined benefit pension scheme, the amount of accrued retirement benefits (excluding money purchase benefits or those from his own voluntary contributions).

- Whether he/she exercised share options or received or became entitled to shares under a long-term incentive scheme (non-listed companies only).

Finally, disclose excess retirement benefits paid to directors or past directors, and compensation for loss of office, including payments in connection with breach of contract.

Interest payable

Disclose the amount of interest payable, analysed between interest payable on:

- bank loans and overdrafts
- other loans.

Disclose the amount of interest capitalised.

Tax on profit on ordinary activities

Disclose any special circumstances affecting the tax liability.

Dividends

Disclose the total amount paid and proposed.

Prior year items

Disclose the effect of amounts included in the profit and loss account relating to previous years.

Disclose prior period adjustments (per FRS 3) shown as adjustments to retained earnings brought forward.

5 *Preparing company accounts*

Prepare a sheet for the profit and loss account, a separate sheet for the balance sheet, a sheet for notes to the accounts and a sheet for workings.

Let the format dictate the order of working. Work through the profit and loss account picking up the information as you go.

Then prepare the balance sheet using exactly the same approach. Allow the format to take you through the question.

6 *Directors' report*

Contents are specified by Companies Acts.

In assessment questions "financial statements" does not include a directors' report – therefore only produce one if specifically asked for.

7 Summary financial statements

SFS may be produced by public limited companies which have a full Stock Exchange Listing as an alternative to producing full accounts.

- Companies must always file a full set of accounts with the Registrar of Companies.
- Contents of the summary financial statements must be derived from the full accounts. No additional information can be included which is not in the full accounts.

8 Abbreviated accounts

Small and medium-sized companies are allowed to prepare two sets of accounts: normal full accounts for their shareholders and abbreviated accounts which are filed at Companies House.

Qualifying conditions

- At least two to be satisfied for the current and immediately preceding financial years.

		Small	*Medium*
1	**Turnover** not more than:	£2,800,000	£11,200,000
2	**Assets** not more than:	£1,400,000	£5,600,000
3	**Average number of employees** not more than:	50	250

- If the qualifying conditions are met, the company will be entitled to the same status in the following financial year irrespective of whether the criteria are met then.
- If the qualifying conditions are met in the company's first financial year, it can file abbreviated accounts in that year.

Exemptions permitted for medium-sized companies

- No requirement to state whether the accounts have been prepared in accordance with applicable accounting standards.
- **Profit and loss account**
  - Start with gross profit (ie no figures for turnover and cost of sales need to be disclosed).
  - No analysis of turnover by class of business or geographical destination.

Exemptions permitted for small-sized companies

- No requirement to state whether the accounts have been prepared in accordance with applicable accounting standards.
- **Profit and loss account**

  Not required.
- **Balance sheet**

  Only the figures for the main headings (fixed assets, current assets, etc).
- **Notes to the accounts**

  Only the following notes are required:
  - accounting policies;
  - share capital;
  - debtors recoverable after more than one year;
  - creditors due after more than five years;
  - secured creditors;
  - the movements (in total) on intangible fixed assets, tangible fixed assets and fixed asset investments.
- **Directors' report**

  Not required.

CHAPTER 6

Cash flow statements

1 FRS 1: Cash flow statements

The conventional profit and loss account and balance sheet are drawn up according to the rules of accruals accounting.

Accruals accounting requires judgement in regard to areas such as:

- stock valuation
- depreciation policy
- provision for doubtful debts.

This makes it difficult to interpret a company's results with confidence. Cash flows are less subject to manipulation.

Standard headings in an FRS 1 cash flow statement

- Net cash flow from operating activities
- Dividends from associates (not examinable)
- Returns on investments and servicing of finance
- Taxation
- Capital expenditure
- Acquisitions and disposals (not examinable)
- Equity dividends paid
- Management of liquid resources
- Financing
- Increase/decrease in cash.

Proforma cash flow statement for the year ended 31 December 20X6

	£000	£000
Net cash flow from operating activities (Note 1)		X
Returns on investments and servicing of finance		
Interest received	X	
Interest paid	(X)	
		X
Taxation		(X)
Capital expenditure		
Payments to acquire intangible fixed assets	(X)	
Payments to acquire tangible fixed assets	(X)	
Receipts from sale of tangible fixed assets	X	
		(X)
Equity dividends paid		(X)
Management of liquid resources		
Purchase of treasury bills	(X)	
Sale of treasury bills	X	
		(X)
Financing		
Issue of ordinary share capital	X	
Repurchase of debenture loan	(X)	
Expenses paid in connection with share issue	(X)	
		X
Increase in cash		X

Three notes are also required by FRS 1.

1 *Reconciliation of operating profit to net cash flow from operating activities*

	£000
Operating profit	X
Depreciation charges	X
Increase in stocks	(X)
Increase in debtors	(X)
Increase in creditors	X
Net cash inflow from operating activities	X

2 *Reconciliation of net cash flow to movement in net debt*

	£000	£000
Increase in cash in the period	X	
Cash to repurchase debenture	X	
Cash used to increase liquid resources	X	
Change in net debt		X
Net debt at 1 January 20X6		(X)
Net funds at 31 December 20X6		X

3 *Analysis of changes in net debt*

	At 1 January 20X6 £000	*Cash flows* £000	*Other changes* £000	*At 31 Dec 20X6* £000
Cash in hand and bank	X	X		X
Overdrafts	(X)	X		–
Long-term debt	(X)	X		(X)
Current asset investments	X	X		X
Total	(X)	X		X

2 The elements of a cash flow statement

Net cash flow from operating activities

- Start with the operating profit shown in the profit and loss account.
- Adjust for transactions not involving the movement of cash.
- This reconciliation from operating profit to operating cash flow can be shown as note 1 to the cash flow statement.

Returns on investments and servicing of finance: include dividends received here, whilst equity dividends paid are disclosed separately, lower down the cash flow statement.

Taxation: this is tax *paid* during the year, not the tax *charged* in the profit and loss account. The same is true for dividends.

Management of liquid resources: liquid resources are short-term or current asset investments.

Financing will include any or all of the following elements.

- Proceeds of share issues.
- Payments to redeem a loan.
- Proceeds on taking out a new loan.

Increase/decrease in cash: this includes cash in hand plus deposits repayable on demand, less any overdrafts.

3 Preparing a cash flow statement

Direct and indirect methods for calculating the net cash inflow from operating activities

FRS 1 permits either the direct method or the indirect method to be used to calculate the net cash flow from operating activities.

- The *indirect method* begins with operating profit from the profit and loss account and adjusts this figure for non-cash items and for increases and decreases in working capital.
- The *direct method* uses the actual trading cash flows to arrive at the net cash flow from operating activities. It is less commonly used.

FRS 1 questions usually appear in the same format: you are given two balance sheets plus additional information.

To tackle these questions, work down the balance sheets identifying the movements between the two and then decide where each movement should be disclosed: on the cash flow statement or the notes (or sometimes both).

When you have dealt with a line on the balance sheet, tick it off.

Note 3 has four columns. For each element of net debt, put the opening balance sheet amount in column one, the closing balance sheet amount in column four and the difference in columns two and three.

Note 2 is simply a summary of the information produced in Note 3. The movement or change column is produced first with the cash and overdraft movement being combined and the current asset investment change and long-term debt change being shown separately. Note that all Note 2 figures can be taken from Note 3, so make sure that you prepare Note 3 first.

CHAPTER 7

Consolidated accounts – balance sheet

1 The nature of group accounts

One company (P) owns more than 50% of the ordinary shares of another company (S): usually, P can control S as a result. P is called a parent company and S is called a subsidiary. P and S are distinct legally, but in substance form a group.

Key purpose of group accounts: to reflect the economic substance of the relationship.

Group accounts are *additional* to individual company accounts.

Main method of preparation: consolidated accounts presenting the group as a 'single economic entity'.

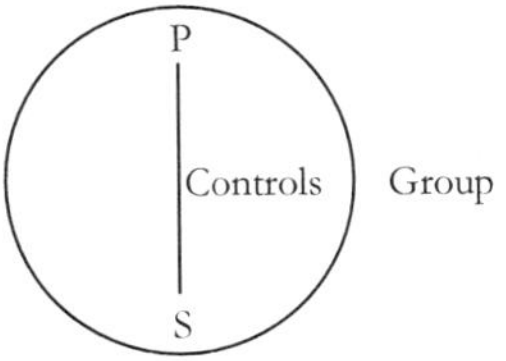

Standard group accounting question: prepare consolidated accounts from individual companies' accounts. Use five standard workings.

(W1) Group structure

(W2) Net assets of S, at date of acquisition and at balance sheet date (net assets equals share capital plus reserves)

(W3) Goodwill

(W4) Minority interest

(W5) Group profit and loss account

2 Buying shares in another company

P buys shares in S: record the cash paid as an investment in P's balance sheet.

Key points in preparing a consolidated balance sheet.

- We include 100% of the assets and liabilities of both the parent and subsidiary because by definition we control these net assets.

- The investment in S will *never* appear in the consolidated balance sheet.
- The share capital of S will *never* appear in the consolidated balance sheet.
- The investment in S is cancelled against the share capital and pre-acquisition reserves on consolidation. The difference (goodwill) appears in the consolidated balance sheet.

Example

Draft balance sheets of Polar and Squirrel on 31 December 20X1 are as follows.

	Polar Ltd	*Squirrel Ltd*
	£000	*£000*
Tangible fixed assets	90	80
Investment in Squirrel at cost	110	
Current assets	50	30
	250	110
Creditors: amounts falling due within one year	(30)	(10)
Total assets less current liabilities	220	100
Capital and reserves		
Share capital	100	100
Profit and loss account	120	-
	220	100

Polar Ltd had just bought 100% of the shares of Squirrel on the balance sheet date.

Required

Prepare a consolidated balance sheet as at 31 December 20X1.

Solution

P controls S and therefore we need to prepare group accounts. P has paid more than book value for S's net assets: there will be an intangible asset 'goodwill' in the group balance sheet.

Polar Group consolidated balance sheet as at 31 December 20X1

	£000	£000
Goodwill (110–100)		10
Tangible fixed assets (90 + 80) [100% (P + S)]		170
		180
Current assets (50 + 30) [100% (P + S)]	80	
Creditors: amounts due within one year (30 + 10) [100% (P + S)]	(40)	
Net current assets		40
Total assets less current liabilities		220
Capital and reserves		
Share capital (100% P only)		100
Profit and loss reserve (100% P)		120
		220

3 *Minority interests*

Any holding of more than 50% of the equity shares is usually sufficient to give control. If we own more than 50%, but less than 100%, of the equity shares there is a minority interest.

Example

Suppose that Polar's investment in Squirrel represents only 80% of Squirrel's equity, not 100%. All other details remain the same.

Required

Prepare a consolidated balance sheet as at 31 December 20X1.

Solution

We own 80% of the shares of Squirrel, so third parties own the rest (20%).

Polar Group consolidated balance sheet as at 31 December 20X1

	£000	£000
Fixed assets		
Intangible assets (110–80)		30
Tangible assets (90 + 80)		170
		200
Current assets (50 + 30)	80	
Creditors: amounts falling due within one year (30 + 10)	(40)	
Net current assets		40
Total assets less current liabilities		240
Capital and reserves		
£1 shares (100% P only)		100
Profit and loss reserves (100% P)		120
Shareholders' capital		220
Minority interest (20% of 100)		20
		240

4 Control and ownership

Group accounts reflect both control and ownership, as shown in the following table.

Control and ownership in the consolidated balance sheet

Consolidated balance sheet	£
Net assets	X
(P + S (100%))	
↓	↓
CONTROL	X

OWNERSHIP	
Capital and reserves:	
Share capital (P only)	X
Reserves (P + P% × S post-acq)	X
Owned by P's shareholders	X
Minority interests (MI% × S's net assets)	X
	X

(Ownership: P% = P's share
MI% = MI share)

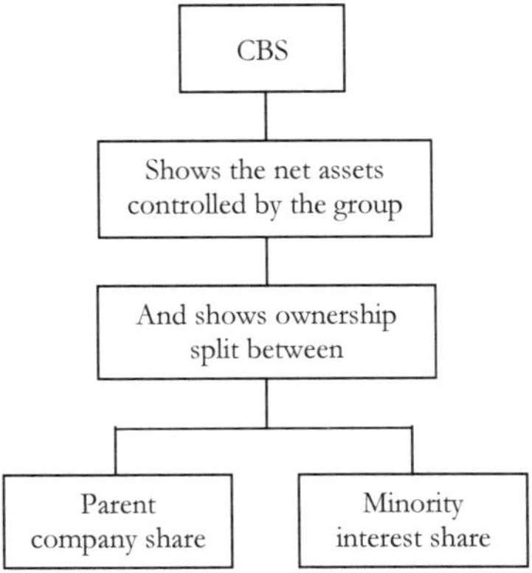

5 Accounting for reserves

The reserves of S when S is acquired are called its 'pre-acquisition' reserves. These are capitalised at the date of acquisition by including them in the goodwill calculation.

Profits earned by S after the date of acquisition are called 'post-acquisition reserves'. Include the group's share of the subsidiaries' post-acquisition reserves in the consolidated balance sheet.

If the subsidiary has other reserves (eg a revaluation reserve, a share premium, a general reserve) use the same basic calculation for each reserve separately.

6 Summary of calculations for CBS

Goodwill

	£
Cost of investment (in P's books)	X
Less: Net assets of S acquired (P's share of S's share capital and reserves at the date of acquisition)	(X)
Goodwill purchased (to be amortised)	X

Minority interests

	£
MI's share of S's net assets at the balance sheet date	X

Consolidated reserves

	£
P's reserves	X
Plus: P's share of S's post-acquisition reserves	X
Less: Goodwill amortised to date	(X)
Group reserves in CBS	X

7 The treatment of goodwill

The requirements of FRS 10

- The amount of goodwill should be the difference between the fair value of the consideration given and the fair value of the separable net assets acquired.
- No amount should be attributed to non-purchased goodwill in accounts.
- Show purchased goodwill as an asset on the balance sheet.
- Show negative goodwill as a negative asset in the fixed assets section of the balance sheet, just below any positive goodwill.
- Charge amortisation in the profit and loss account over the estimated useful life of the goodwill (usually not more than 20 years).
- At the end of the first full year after the acquisition perform a limited impairment review (or a full impairment review if the useful life is more than 20 years).

Example

Balance sheets at 31 December 20X9

	Faye Ltd		Garbo Ltd	
	£	£	£	£
Fixed assets				
Tangible assets		33,000		20,000
Investments: shares in Garbo Ltd at cost		12,000		
Current assets	5,000		15,000	
Creditors: amounts falling due within one year	(9,000)		(10,000)	
Net current (liabilities)/assets		(4,000)		5,000
Total assets less current liabilities		41,000		25,000
Creditors: amounts falling due after more than one year				
8% Debenture loans		20,000		9,000
		21,000		16,000
Capital and reserves				
Called up share capital (£1 ordinary shares)		10,000		4,000
Share premium account		5,000		–
Profit and loss account		6,000		12,000
		21,000		16,000

On 1 January 20X3 Faye Ltd acquired 3,000 shares of Garbo Ltd. At that date the balance on Garbo Ltd's profit and loss account was £8,000.

Required

Prepare the consolidated balance sheet of Faye Ltd at 31 December 20X9, assuming the group policy is to amortise goodwill arising on consolidation over a period of ten years.

Solution

Consolidated balance sheet at 31 December 20X9

	£	£
Fixed assets		
Intangible assets: goodwill (12,000 – (75% × 12,000)) × $\frac{3}{10}$		900
Tangible assets		53,000
Current assets	20,000	
Creditors: amounts falling due within one year	(19,000)	
Net current assets		1,000
Total assets less current liabilities		54,900
Creditors: amounts falling due after more than one year		
8% Debenture loans		(29,000)
		25,900
Capital and reserves		
Called up share capital		10,000
Share premium account		5,000
Profit and loss account (6,000 – 2,100 + (75% × (12,000 – 8,000)))		6,900
		21,900
Minority interest (25% × 16,000)		4,000
		25,900

8 Intra-group balances

When consolidating we need to cancel out items which are assets in one group company and liabilities in another.

This is an application of the single entity concept.

Loans and debentures

This is where one company in the group has made a loan to another. In one company there is a creditor and in the other a debtor. The cancellation process is very simple in that the credit balance of one company is offset against the debit balance of the other company, eliminating both balances from the consolidated balance sheet.

Current accounts

Current accounts are intra-group trading balances. The treatment of current accounts is the same as for loans. However, inter-company current accounts may not agree.

For example, the following balances appeared in the books of P Ltd and S Ltd in their balance sheets dated 31 December 20X0:

	Books of P Ltd	*Books of S Ltd*
	£	£
Current account with S Ltd	10,700 Dr	
Current account with P Ltd		10,000 Cr

On 31 December 20X0 S Ltd had sent a cheque for £700 to P Ltd which the latter company did not record until 2 January 20X1. This is called cash-in-transit.

The necessary consolidation adjustment will be to follow the transaction to its natural conclusion by recording the receipt of the cash in P Ltd's books, thus decreasing its current account balance by £700 to £10,000, and increasing its cash balance by £700. The current account balances of £10,000 can then be cancelled out.

9 Dividends

Individual companies

If a subsidiary proposes a dividend, the effects will be as follows:

- Subsidiary company books:

Dr Profit and loss	X	
Cr Dividend creditor		X

  with the dividend payable.

- Parent company books:

Dr Dividend debtor	X	
Cr Profit and loss account		X

  with its share of the dividend receivable from the subsidiary company.

Consolidation adjustment

The dividend debtor in the parent company's books is receivable from another group company, and should be cancelled out against all (if 100% owned) or part (if less than 100% owned) of the dividend creditor in the subsidiary company's books. Any balance left on the dividend creditor of the subsidiary company represents the dividend owed to the minority shareholders of the company.

The only figure that will appear in the consolidated net assets will be any dividend payable by the subsidiary to the minority shareholders.

10 Unrealised intra-group profit

Where, during the period under review, goods (or any other assets) are transferred between group companies at prices other than cost, the transferring company can make a profit.

In consolidated accounts, we want to reflect only profits made by group companies trading with third parties (single entity concept).

No adjustment is necessary on consolidation if the goods (or assets) have been sold on, outside the group, within the period. However, where such goods (or assets) are still held within the group at the end of the accounting period, the consolidated accounts would not show a true and fair view of the profits of the group as a whole if the profits made on such transfers were not eliminated.

Stocks

The adjustment for the unrealised profit on stocks is straightforward where the parent company sells goods to the subsidiary. The profit is made by the parent and recorded in its books. Hence, it is all owned by the parent.

Example

During the current accounting period P Ltd transferred goods to S Ltd for £12,000, which gave P Ltd a profit of £3,000. One third of these goods were included in the stocks of S Ltd at the balance sheet date.

What consolidation adjustment is required?

Solution

The adjustment in the consolidated balance sheet would be as follows:

		£	£
Dr	Profit and loss account (⅓ × £3,000)	1,000	
	Cr Balance sheet stocks		1,000

The stock of goods still held by S Ltd, valued at £4,000 in S's stock, is being reduced to its cost to the group of £3,000.

Sales of goods from subsidiary to parent company

On the net assets side of the balance sheet, the unrealised profit is still eliminated from stocks in full. This is because the group as a whole has bought and is holding stock, which should therefore be shown at the lower of cost and net realisable value to the group. The profit on the sale will have been recorded in the subsidiary's books. On consolidation, the adjustment to eliminate this is apportioned between the parent and minority interests according to the ownership interests in the subsidiary.

Example

During the current accounting period S Ltd sold goods to P Ltd for £18,000 which gave S Ltd a profit of £6,000. At the balance sheet date half of these goods are included in P Ltd's stock. P owns 80% of S.

What consolidation adjustment is required?

Solution

The adjustment in the consolidated balance sheet would be as follows:

	£	£
Dr Group profit and loss account (½ × 6,000 × 80%)	2,400	
Dr Minority interest (½ × 6,000 × 20%)	600	
Cr Balance sheet stocks (½ × 6,000)		3,000

11 Fair values

Goodwill is determined by comparing the value of the business as a whole with the aggregate of the fair values of its identifiable net assets.

If the fair value of the subsidiary's net assets, at the date of acquisition, is different from their book value, the book amounts should be **adjusted to fair value on consolidation.**

Example

Hardy Ltd acquired 80% of the share capital of Woolf Ltd for £54,000 on 31 December 20X7. The draft balance sheets of the two companies have been drawn up on that date.

	Hardy Ltd £	*Woolf Ltd* £
Fixed assets		
Tangible assets	75,000	35,000
Investment in Woolf Ltd	54,000	–
Current assets	35,000	39,500
Creditors: Amounts falling due within one year	(42,000)	(16,000)
	122,000	58,500
Share capital – £1 ordinary shares	60,000	20,000
Profit and loss account	62,000	38,500
	122,000	58,500

You are given the following additional information:

The fair value of the net assets of Woolf Ltd, on 31 December 20X7, was £66,000. This increase can be attributed to freehold land.

Required

Prepare the consolidated balance sheet of Hardy Ltd as at 31 December 20X7.

Solution

Fair value adjustment

Looking at the net assets of Woolf Ltd:

	£
Fair value at 31 December 20X7	66,000
Book value at 31 December 20X7	58,500
Revaluation	7,500

We must increase the book value of Woolf Ltd's freehold land by £7,500. The necessary journal entry is:

	£	£
Dr Fixed assets – freehold land	7,500	
Cr Revaluation reserve		7,500

The increase in the value of Woolf Ltd's land occurred over time up to the date of takeover. The revaluation reserve is therefore a **pre–acquisition** reserve and is treated in the same way as pre–acquisition profits.

We will now prepare the consolidated balance sheet.

Hardy Ltd: Consolidated balance sheet at 31 December 20X7

	£
Fixed assets:	
Intangible assets: goodwill (W3)	1,200
Tangible assets (75 + 42.5)	117,500
Current assets (35 + 39.5)	74,500
Creditors: Amounts falling due within one year (42 + 16)	(58,000)
	135,200
Share capital – £1 ordinary shares	60,000
Profit and loss account	62,000
	122,000
Minority interest (W4)	13,200
	135,200

Consolidation workings

(W1) Group structure

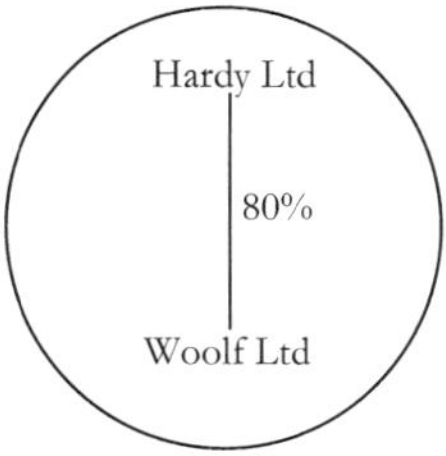

(W2) Net assets of Woolf at 31 December 20X7

	£
Share capital	20,000
Profit and loss account	38,500
	58,500
Revaluation reserve	7,500
Fair value of net assets	66,000

(W3) Goodwill schedule

	£
Cost of shares in Woolf	54,000
Net assets acquired (80% × 66,000) (W2)	52,800
	1,200

(W4) Minority interest schedule

	£
20% × 66,000 (W2)	13,200

(Note that there are no post-acquisition profits for the subsidiary, and no need to amortise the goodwill since the acquisition has only just taken place.)

12 Other considerations

Other reserves

A subsidiary may have other reserves in its balance sheet, such as a revaluation reserve. On consolidation, we treat these in exactly the same way as the profit and loss reserve. Hence, the reserves at acquisition are taken to the goodwill computation and the parent's share of any post-acquisition reserves is added to the parent's own reserves.

Accounting policies

If a subsidiary uses different accounting policies in preparing its own accounts from those adopted by the group as a whole (eg regarding development costs), the subsidiary's accounts should be adjusted prior to consolidation for consistency.

Goodwill in a subsidiary's own books

We calculate goodwill on consolidation based on the fair value of the subsidiary's separable net assets acquired. Any goodwill recorded in the subsidiary's own balance sheet is not an asset separable from the business as a whole. Hence we need to eliminate this goodwill by adjusting the subsidiary's net assets prior to consolidating.

CHAPTER 8

Consolidated accounts – profit and loss account

1 Accounting for subsidiary companies

Include in the CPL all of S's income and expenses (100%), line by line, down to and including profit after tax (even if the parent's equity share in S is less than 100%).

Then adjust for any minority interest in S's profits by deducting the appropriate share of S's profits after tax as a separate line in the CPL. The balance of profit remaining at this stage is the profit attributable to P's shareholders.

Exclude dividends payable by S to P from P's individual profit and loss account before consolidating.

- Any dividends paid or proposed in the CPL are the dividends paid by P to P's shareholders.
- Any dividend income shown in the CPL must arise from trade investments, *not* investments in S.

Exclude any other intra-group trading.

- Add across P and S turnover and cost of sales to get the consolidated figure.
- Deduct the value of the inter-company sale from consolidated turnover and cost of sales.
- If any items sold by one group company to another are included in closing stocks, their value must be adjusted to the lower of cost and net realisable value to the group.

Below is illustrated the CPL for a parent company with an 80% subsidiary.

Consolidated profit and loss account for the year ended ……

	£000	£000
Turnover (100% of P and S, less inter-company sales)		X
Cost of sales (100% of P and S, less inter-company sales plus unrealised profit in stock)		(X)
Gross profit (100% of P and S, less unrealised profit in stock)		X
Distribution costs (100% of P and S)		(X)
Administrative expenses (100% of P and S)		(X)
Operating profit		X
Investment income (external only)		X
Profit before tax (cast down)		X
Taxation (100% of P and S)		(X)
Profit after tax (cast down)		X
Less: Minority interests (20% of S's profit after tax)		(X)
Profit attributable to members of P (cast down)		X
Dividends (100% of P only)		(X)
Retained profit (cast down)		X
Retained profit brought forward		
100% P	X	
+80% of S's post-acquisition profit	X	
Less: Goodwill amortised	(X)	
		X
Retained profit carried forward (cast down)		X

Example

Given below are the profit and loss accounts for P plc and its subsidiary L Ltd for the year ended 31 December 20X5.

	P plc	*L Ltd*
	£000	£000
Turnover	3,200	2,560
Cost of sales	(2,200)	(1,480)
Gross profit	1,000	1,080
Distribution costs	(160)	(120)
Administrative expenses	(400)	(80)
	440	880
Investment income	160	–
	600	880
Taxation	(400)	(480)
Profit on ordinary activities after tax	200	400
Dividend	(96)	(200)
Retained profit for year	104	200
Retained profit brought forward	1,200	1,120
Retained profit carried forward	1,304	1,320

- P plc paid £1.5 million on 31 December 20X1 for 80% of L Ltd's share capital of £800,000. The balance on L Ltd's profit and loss account was £600,000 at that time. Goodwill has been fully amortised.
- P plc made sales to L Ltd which were worth a total of £600,000 during the year. Not all of the goods had been resold by the year end. The profit element included in L Ltd's closing stock was £30,000.
- The figure for investment income in P plc's profit statement comprises the parent company's share of the subsidiary's total dividend for the year.

Required

Prepare a consolidated profit and loss account for the year ended 31 December 20X5 for the P group.

Solution

Consolidated profit and loss account of P plc for the year ended 31 December 20X5

	£000
Turnover (3,200 + 2,560 – 600)	5,160
Cost of sales (2,200 + 1,480 – 600 + 30))	(3,110)
Gross profit (1,000 + 1,080 – 30)	2,050
Distribution costs (160 + 120)	(280)
Administrative expenses (400 + 80)	(480)
Profit on ordinary activities before tax	1,290
Taxation (400 + 480)	(880)
Profit on ordinary activities after tax	410
Less minority interests (400 × 20%)	(80)
Group profit after tax (cast down)	330
Dividends (100% P only)	(96)
Retained profit for the year	234
Retained profit brought forward (1,200 + (80% × 520) – 380 (W))	1,236
Retained profit carried forward	1,470

Working

Goodwill = £1.5m – 80% (£800,000 + £600,000)

= £380,000

CHAPTER 9

Consolidated accounts – legal and professional requirements

1 Companies Act 1985 requirements

Definition of parent and subsidiary

The full definition is given in the Companies Act and is restated in FRS 2. The key points of the definition are summarised below:

An undertaking is the parent of another (a subsidiary) if *any* of the following apply:

- It holds a majority of voting rights.
- It is a member and can appoint/remove directors with a majority of votes.
- It is a member and controls a majority of votes via an agreement with other members.
- It has a participating interest and actually exercises dominant influence or the undertakings are managed on a unified basis.

FRS 2 defines *dominant influence*. In essence, the term means that the parent determines the financial and operating policies of the subsidiary, which effectively means that the parent has control.

FRS 2 also defines *managed on a unified basis*. This term means that the undertakings are integrated and managed as a single unit.

Exemptions from the requirement to prepare group accounts

A company need not prepare group accounts if:

- its immediate parent is incorporated in the European Union (EU) and prepares accounts in accordance with (EU) requirements; and
- the company seeking the exemption does not have any securities listed on a stock exchange in the EU; and
- the company is a wholly owned subsidiary of its immediate parent; or
- the parent owns over 50%, and notice requiring group accounts has not been served by:
  - holders of more than half of the remaining shares *not* held by the parent; or
  - holders of 5% of total shares.

Small and medium-sized groups exemptions

A small or medium-sized group, not containing a public company, a banking, authorised investment or insurance company, need not prepare group accounts if it:

- meets any two of the small/medium-size limits for two consecutive years; or
- met size criteria and was entitled to exemption last year; or
- meets size criteria this year and was entitled to exemption last year.

Size limits:

	Before consolidation adjustments		*After consolidation adjustments*
Turnover not more than	£13,440,000	or	£11,200,000
Gross assets not more than	£6,720,000	or	£5,600,000
Average number of employees not more than		250	

- The totals before consolidation adjustments are obtained by adding together the amounts in the individual company accounts.
- The totals after consolidation adjustments are obtained from the group balance sheet and profit and loss account.

2 *FRS 2: Accounting for subsidiary undertakings*

Objective of FRS 2

The objective of FRS 2 is to require parent undertakings to provide financial information about their group in consolidated financial statements, intended to present the parent and its subsidiaries as a single economic entity.

Minority interests

The consolidated balance sheet should show separately the minority interest share of the subsidiary's net assets or liabilities consolidated.

The consolidated profit and loss account should show separately the minority interest share of the subsidiary's profit or loss after tax for the period.

Intra-group transactions

Eliminate in full any profits or losses on intra-group transactions reflected in the book value of assets included in consolidation.

Apportion the elimination of profits or losses between the parent and minority interests in proportion to their holdings in the company recording the profit or loss in its own financial statements.

Changes in composition of a group

Changes in membership of a group occur on the date on which control passes.

3 *Associated undertakings*

A group of companies consists of P and its subsidiaries. P controls each S by holding more than 50% of the equity.

An associated undertaking (A) is defined as an entity over which the group exercises significant influence, but not control. If the group holds 20% or more of the company's equity we assume that significant influence exists.

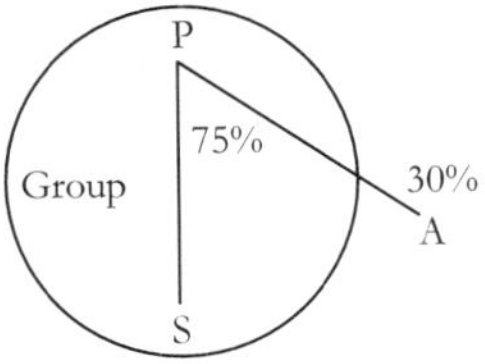

The shares in A may be owned either by P or by S.

FRS 9 requires the use of the equity method to account for associates in the consolidated accounts. The investing group must disclose its share of associates':

- operating profit or loss
- non-operating exceptional items
- interest receivable and payable
- tax charge.

The investing group must also disclose the amortisation of goodwill on the acquisition of A.

In the investing company's individual accounts the balance sheet shows participating interests as a fixed asset investment, stated (usually) at cost. The individual company's profit and loss account shows dividend income received from associates under the heading 'income from participating interests'.

In the consolidated accounts we use the equity accounting method and refer to A as an associated undertaking.

The main steps in equity accounting – balance sheet

- Replace the fixed asset investment shown in the individual company balance sheet with the group share of A's net assets at the balance sheet date, in one line. The caption is 'Interests in associated undertakings'.
- In group reserves, include P's share of A's post-acquisition reserves.

- Cancel the investment in A in the individual company's books against the share of A's net assets acquired (at fair value). The difference is a premium or discount on acquisition (goodwill).
- Calculate goodwill and present it within the 'investments in associates' caption (separately disclosed).

Example

Below are the balance sheets of three companies as at 31 December 20X9.

		Dipsy Ltd	*LaaLaa Ltd*	*Po Ltd*
		£000	£000	£000
Fixed assets				
Tangible assets		1,120	980	840
Investments	672,000 shares in LaaLaa	644	–	–
	168,000 shares in Po	224	–	–
Current assets		605	1,008	336
Creditors: amounts falling due within one year		(353)	(588)	(196)
		2,240	1,400	980
Capital and reserves				
£1 ordinary shares		1,120	840	560
Profit and loss account		1,120	560	420
		2,240	1,400	980

You are also given the following information.

- Dipsy Ltd acquired its shares in LaaLaa Ltd a number of years ago when LaaLaa Ltd had a debit balance on its profit and loss account of £56,000.
- Dipsy Ltd acquired its shares in Po Ltd a number of years ago when Po Ltd had a credit balance on its profit and loss account of £140,000.
- Creditors include the final proposed dividends of the three companies, which are as follows.

Dipsy Ltd	£112,000
LaaLaa Ltd	£42,000
Po Ltd	£28,000

- Dipsy Ltd has not accounted for any dividends receivable.
- Goodwill is fully amortised.

Required

Prepare workings for the consolidated balance sheet as at 31 December 20X9 for Dipsy Ltd and its subsidiary, incorporating its associated company in accordance with FRS 9.

Solution

Adjust for the dividends which have not been accounted for (on the face of the question paper).

Then prepare the net assets working in the normal way. For the associate, the working is as follows.

1 Net assets - Po

	At date of acquisition	*At balance sheet date*
	£000	£000
£1 shares	560	560
Profit and loss account	140	420
	700	980

Then calculate goodwill on acquisition as usual. For the associate the working is as follows.

2 Goodwill – Po

	£000
Purchase consideration	224
For 30% of net assets (£700,000)	(210)
Goodwill	14

Calculate minority interest in the subsidiary only.

In the group profit and loss account reserve, include our share of the post-acquisition reserves of the associate just as we do for a subsidiary.

3 Group profit and loss account

	£000
100% Dipsy	1,120.0
Dividends	
From LaaLaa	33.6
From Po	8.4
	1,162.0
Laa Laa 560,000 – (£56,000) Pre-acquisition	
Laa Laa 560,000 – Post–acquisition £616,000 × 80%	492.8
Po 420,000 – £140,000 Pre-acquisition	
Po 420,000 – Post–acquisition £280,000 × 30%	84.0
Less: Goodwill fully amortised	
Laa Laa (£644,000 – (80% × £784,000))	(16.8)
Po	(14.0)
	1,708.0

Then calculate the investment in the associated company.

4 Investment in associated company

Share of net assets (£980,000 × 30%)	£294,000

When we consolidate we have to remember that the dividend debtor from the associate does not cancel on consolidation - it is not part of the group.

Equity accounting in the consolidated profit and loss account

The main steps are as follows.

- The investing company's individual profit and loss account includes dividend income from the investment in A. In the CPL, replace this with the group's share of A's operating profit, and disclose it as 'income from interests in associated undertakings'.

- Include the group's share of A's tax charge in the group tax charge, and disclose the amount separately in a note to the accounts.
- If A was acquired in mid-year, time-apportion its profit or loss.
- Do not cancel inter-company balances and trading with A, as A is not part of the group.
- For dividends from A, ensure that dividends payable and receivable are fully accounted for in the books of the individual companies. The consolidated balance sheet will show a debtor for dividends due to the group from A.
- Eliminate unrealised profit on sales from P to A or A to P by adjusting the net assets of A so as to eliminate profit prior to equity accounting.

Example

Below are the profit and loss accounts of the Barbie group and its associated company, as at 31 December 20X8.

	Barbie plc	*Ken Ltd*	*Shelly Ltd*
	£000	£000	£000
Turnover	385	100	60
Cost of sales	(185)	(60)	(20)
Gross profit	200	40	40
Expenses	(50)	(15)	(10)
Profit before tax	150	25	30
Tax	(50)	(12)	(10)
Profit after tax	100	13	20
Dividends	(40)	–	(10)
Retained profit for the year	60	13	10
Retained profit brought forward	190	60	140
Retained profit carried forward	250	73	150

You are also given the following information.

- Barbie plc acquired 60,000 shares in Shelly Ltd for £80,000 when that company had a credit balance on its profit and loss account of £50,000 a number of years ago. Shelly Ltd has 200,000 £1 ordinary shares.
- Barbie plc acquired 45,000 shares in Ken Ltd for £70,000 when that company's profit and loss reserves were £20,000. Ken Ltd has 50,000 £1 ordinary shares.

- The dividends of Barbie and Shelly are final proposed dividends and Barbie plc has not accounted for any dividends receivable.
- Any goodwill has been fully amortised.

Solution

Consolidated profit and loss account for the year ended 31 December 20X8

	£000	£000
Turnover (385 + 100)		485.0
Cost of sales (185 + 60)		(245.0)
Gross profit (200 + 40)		240.0
Administrative expenses (50 + 15)		(65.0)
Share of profits of associated company (30% of Shelly's operating profit)		9.0
Profit before tax		184.0
Taxation: group (50 + 12)		(62.0)
Shelly (30% × 10)		(3.0)
Profit after tax		119.0
Minority interest (10% of Ken's profit after tax)		(1.3)
Profit attributable to members of Barbie		117.7
Dividends (Barbie only, 100%)		(40.0)
Retained profit for the year		77.7
Barbie	190	
Ken (60 – 20) × 90%	36	
Shelly (140 – 50) × 30%	27	
Goodwill fully amortised (70 – (90% × 70)) + (80 – (30% × 250))	(12)	
Retained profit brought forward		241.0
Retained profit carried forward		318.7

4 *Acquisition accounting and merger accounting*

Common features of an acquisition

- P pays out cash and the resources of the group are reduced accordingly.
- There is a change of ownership.

However, there are some business combinations which do not have the substance of an acquisition.

Suppose that A plc wishes to purchase shares in B plc. The situation *before* this transaction is as follows.

Before

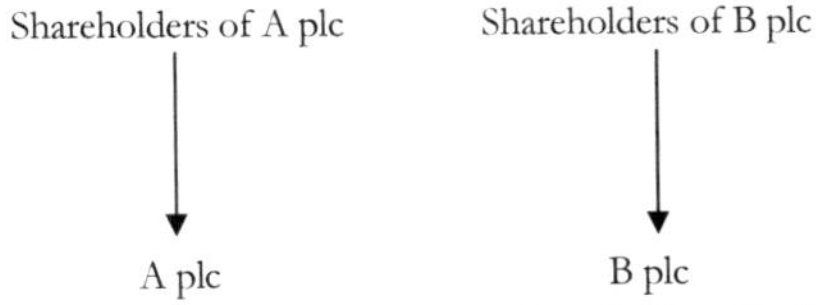

A plc now acquires the entire share capital of B plc from B plc's shareholders and pays for them by issuing shares in A plc in exchange. The situation now looks like this:

After

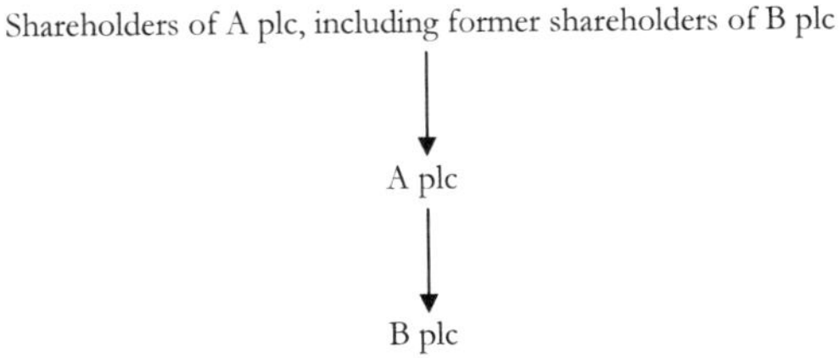

In this scenario the key features of an acquisition are missing.

- B plc's former shareholders retain an interest in the group after the merger.
- A plc has not paid out resources (ie cash) in exchange for B plc.

FRS 6 requires that a merger should be accounted for using merger accounting to produce the consolidated financial statements, rather than conventional acquisition accounting.

Key features of merger accounting

- The net assets of the combining parties need not be adjusted to fair value.
- Profits/losses and cash flows are consolidated from the start of the accounting period in which the combination occurs, even if the merger was in mid-year. Comparatives are restated to achieve uniformity.
- The difference between the nominal value of equity shares issued (plus the fair value of any other consideration) and the nominal value of shares acquired in exchange is shown as a movement on reserves in the group accounts.

Sources of regulations on merger accounting

- The Companies Act 1985, Schedule 4A.
- FRS 6 *Acquisitions and Mergers.*

Requirements for a combination to be treated as a merger: CA requirements:

- After the combination at least 90% of the nominal value of shares carrying unrestricted rights to participate in distributions (and in assets on liquidation) is held by or on behalf of the parent or its subsidiaries.
- The shareholding was attained through an arrangement providing for the issue of equity shares by a parent or its subsidiaries.
- The fair value of any consideration other than the issue of equity shares is not greater than 10% of the nominal value of equity shares issued.
- Adoption of the merger method of accounting accords with generally accepted accounting principles (ie it must comply with FRS 6).

FRS 6 criteria

- Criterion 1: No party to the combination is portrayed as acquirer or acquiree.
- Criterion 2: All parties to the combination participate in establishing the management structure, and decisions are made by consensus.
- Criterion 3: Relative sizes are not so disparate that one entity dominates by virtue of size.
- Criterion 4: Consideration
    - Consideration for equity shares obtained comprises primarily equity shares in the combined entity.
    - Any non-equity consideration is an immaterial proportion of the fair value of consideration.
    - Take into account consideration for equity shares acquired in the two years prior to combination. (This will have been recorded at fair value.)
- Criterion 5: No equity shareholders retain any material interest in the future performance of only part of the combined entity.

If these criteria are satisfied merger accounting *must* be used (unless it would be forbidden by CA 1985).

CHAPTER 10

Reporting financial performance

1 FRS 3: Reporting financial performance

Introduction

The aim of FRS 3 is to improve financial reporting by addressing a number of important issues. These include the following.

- The structure of the profit and loss account.
- Extraordinary items and exceptional items.
- The statement of total recognised gains and losses (STRGL).
- Other required disclosures.

Structure of the profit and loss account

FRS 3 requires that all statutory profit and loss account headings from turnover to operating profit must be analysed between amounts arising from continuing operations and amounts arising from discontinued operations. In addition, turnover and operating profit must be further analysed between amounts from existing and amounts from newly acquired operations. Only the figures for turnover and operating profit need be shown on the face of the profit and loss account. All additional information may be relegated to a note.

The situation is summarised below:

The structure of the profit and loss account under FRS 3

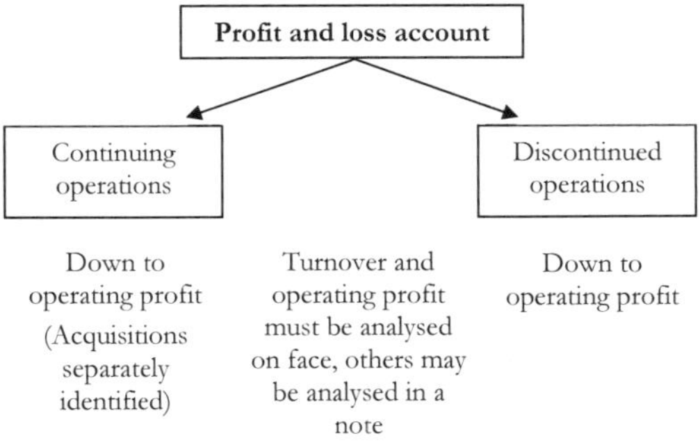

Proforma profit and loss account

X Limited – profit and loss account for the year ended 31 October 20X4

	Continuing operations		*Discontinued*	
	Existing	*Acquisitions*	*operations*	*Total*
	£000	£000	£000	£000
Turnover	550	50	175	775
Cost of sales	(415)	(40)	(165)	(620)
Gross profit	135	10	10	155
Distribution costs	(35)	(4)	(8)	(47)
Administrative expenses	(50)		(7)	(57)
Operating profit	50	6	(5)	51
Profit on sale of properties	22			22
Loss on sale of discontinued operations			(10)	(10)
Profit on ordinary activities before interest	72	6	(15)	63
Interest payable				(18)
Profit on ordinary activities before taxation				45
Tax on profit on ordinary activities				(16)
(Profit before extraordinary items)				29
(Extraordinary items) (to show position only)				–
Profit for the financial year				29
Dividends				(8)
Retained profit for the financial year				21

Discontinued operations are those that meet the following conditions.

- Must have been completed before the earlier of three months after the year end or the date the financial statements are approved.
- Former activity must have ceased permanently.
- Sale or termination has a material effect.
- Assets, liabilities, results of operations and activities are clearly distinguishable.

Three exceptional items must be disclosed on the face of the profit and loss account:

- Profit/loss on sale of discontinued operations
- Costs of restructuring/reorganisation
- Profit/loss on disposal of fixed assets.

FRS 3 virtually abolishes extraordinary items.

As soon as you identify that a task includes discontinued operations, use a four-column layout as follows.

Profit and loss account

Continuing			
Existing	*Acquisition*	*Discontinued*	*Total*
£	£	£	£

FRS 3 achieves a clarification of what is included in the profit figure and generally adds completeness of information.

2 Other disclosures required by FRS 3

Statement of total recognised gains and losses (STRGL): to be presented with the same prominence as the profit and loss account, balance sheet and cash flow statement as a primary statement.

Statement of total recognised gains and losses

		£
(a)	Profit for the financial year (per the profit and loss account)	X
(b)	Items taken directly to reserves	
	Unrealised surplus on revaluation of fixed assets	X
	Surplus/deficit on revaluation of investment properties	X
	Currency translation differences on foreign currency net investments	X
	Total recognised gains and losses for the year	X
	Prior period adjustments	(X)
	Total gains and losses recognised since last annual report	X

The statement will include all gains and losses occurring during the period.

Transactions with shareholders (eg dividends paid) are excluded.

Where profit or loss for the year is the only recognised gain or loss, a statement to that effect should be given immediately below the profit and loss account.

Reconciliation of movements in shareholders' funds: to be included in the notes to the accounts, or it may be a primary statement.

Reconciliation of movements in shareholders' funds

	£
Profit for the financial year	X
Dividends	(X)
Other recognised gains and losses (per STRGL)	X
New share capital	X
Net addition to shareholders' funds	X
Opening shareholders' funds	X
Closing shareholders' funds	X

Example

Kenneth Ltd – profit and loss account extracts for the year ended 31 December 20X1

	£000
Profit after tax	421
Dividend	(98)
Retained profit	323

During the year the following important events took place.

- Assets were revalued by £105,000.
- £250,000 share capital was issued during the year at par.
- Certain stock items were written down by £21,000.
- Opening shareholders' funds were £2,302,000.

Required

Show how the events for the year would be shown in the statement of total recognised gains and losses and the reconciliation of movements in shareholders' funds.

Solution

Statement of total recognised gains and losses

	£000
Profit for the year	421
Asset revaluation	105
Total recognised gains for the year	526

Reconciliation of movements in shareholders' funds

	£000
Profit for the year	421
Dividends	(98)
	323
Other recognised gains and losses	105
New share capital	250
	678
Opening shareholders' funds	2,302
Closing shareholders' funds	2,980

Prior period adjustments

Prior period adjustments arise from:

- changes in accounting policy, or
- correction of fundamental errors.

Distinguish a change in accounting policy from:

- a change in an estimate (eg useful economic life, outcome of development project).
- a refinement of accounting policy (eg if business moves into a new area).

To record a prior period adjustment

- Restate opening balances for the current year and apply the new basis in preparing the current year's accounts.
- Adjust comparative figures.

Note of historical cost profits and losses

If a material difference arises from using revalued amounts in the accounts, then the financial statements must include a reconciliation statement after the statement of recognised gains and losses or the profit and loss account. The profit figure to be reconciled is profit before tax. However, the retained profit for the year must also be restated.

Historical cost vs revaluation

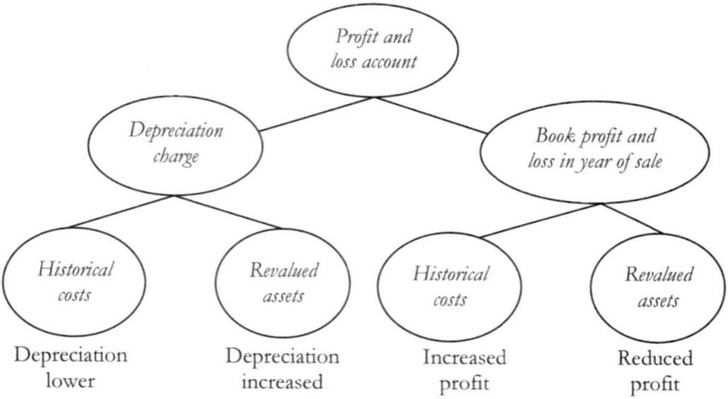

Example

Beta Ltd reported a profit before tax of £705,000 for the year ended 31 December 20X4. During the year the following transactions in fixed assets took place:

An asset with a book value of £70,000 was revalued to £110,000. The remaining useful life is estimated to be five years.

A piece of land which was revalued by £200,000 five years ago was sold to a property developer for £1,200,000, giving a profit of £340,000.

Required

Show the note of historical cost profit for the year ended 31 December 20X4.

Approach to the example

Start with reported profit before tax.

Note of historical cost profits and losses

	£000
Profit before tax per profit and loss account	705
'Excess' depreciation (£110,000 – £70,000)/5	8
Realisation of revaluation surplus	200
Historical cost profit before tax	913

Once an unrealised gain or loss is recognised in the STRGL, transfer for inclusion in the profit and loss account when it becomes realised at a later date is not allowed.

3 SSAP 25: Segmental reporting

SSAP 25 *Segmental reporting* applies to all financial statements intended to give a true and fair view. However the disclosure requirements which go further than statutory requirements only apply to an entity that:

- is a public limited company or a holding company that has a public limited company as a subsidiary; or
- is a banking or insurance company; or
- exceeds the criteria, multiplied in each case by 10, for defining a medium-sized company under S248 CA 1985.

Where, in the opinion of the directors, the disclosure of any information required by SSAP 25 would be seriously prejudicial to the interests of the company, that information need not be disclosed, but the fact that any such information has not been disclosed must be stated.

Definitions

A *class of business* is a distinguishable component of an enterprise that provides a separate product or service or a separate group of related products or services.

A *geographical segment* is a geographical area comprising an individual country or group of countries in which an enterprise operates, or to which it supplies products or services.

Common costs are costs that relate to more than one segment.

How segments should be identified

The directors should determine whether the company has carried on business of two or more classes or has supplied markets that differ substantially from each other. In identifying separate reportable segments, the directors should have regard to the overall purpose of presenting segmental information and the need of the user of the financial statements to be informed where a company carries on operations in different classes of business or in different geographical areas that:

- earn a return on investment that is out of line with the remainder of the business; or
- are subject to different degrees of risk; or
- have experienced different rates of growth; or
- have different potentials for future development.

Disclosure required for each class of business and each geographical segment

- *Turnover*, distinguishing between:
  - turnover derived from external customers; and
  - turnover derived from other segments.

Note that segmental information should be given in terms of the geographical origin of the turnover, rather than the destination. So we are principally showing the geographical segments *from which* the segments were supplied, rather than the segments *to which* they were supplied. Turnover split by destination need only be disclosed if this is materially different from turnover split by source.

- *Segment result*, before accounting for taxation, minority interests and extraordinary items and normally before taking account of interest.
- *Segment net assets*, normally being the non-interest-bearing operating net assets.

The total of the information disclosed by segment should agree with the related figure in the financial statements. If it does not, the company should provide a reconciliation between the two figures.

4 Illustration of SSAP 25 disclosures

Analysis by classes of business

	Industry A	*Industry B*	*Other industries*	*Total*
	£m	£m	£m	£m
Turnover				
Total sales	33	42	26	101
Inter-segment sales	(4)	–	(12)	(16)
Sales to third parties	29	42	14	85
Profit before tax				
Segment profit	3	4.5	1.8	9.3
Common costs				(0.3)
Operating profit				9.0
Net interest				(0.4)
				8.6
Share of associates' profit before tax				2.4
Group profit before tax				11.0
Net assets				
Segment net assets	17.6	24	19.4	61
Unallocated assets				3
				64
Share of associates' net assets				19
Total net assets				83

Analysis by geographical areas

	United Kingdom £m	Far East £m	Other £m	Group £m
Turnover				
Total sales	67	23	12	102
Inter-segment sales	(8)	(9)	–	(17)
Sales to third parties	59	14	12	85
Profit before tax				
Segment profit	6.5	1.8	1.0	9.3
Common costs				(0.3)
Operating profit				9.0
Net interest				(0.4)
				8.6
Share of associates' profit before tax				2.4
Group profit before tax				11.0
Net assets				
Segment net assets	41	16	4	61
Unallocated assets				3
				64
Share of associates' net assets				19
Total net assets				83

5 *FRS 14: Earnings per share*

The basic EPS calculation is simply $\frac{\text{Earnings for year}}{\text{Number of ordinary shares in issue}}$.

Here 'earnings' means group profit after tax, less minority interests and preference dividends.

Example

Gerard plc

Draft profit and loss account for the year ended 31 December 20X4

	£000	£000
Profit before tax		5,060
Taxation		(2,300)
Profit after tax		2,760
Transfer to reserves	230	
Dividends		
Paid - preference interim dividend	276	
Paid - ordinary interim dividend	368	
Proposed - preference final dividend	276	
Proposed - ordinary final dividend	460	1,610
Retained profit		1,150

On 1 January 20X4 the issued share capital of Gerard plc was 9,200,000 6 per cent preference shares of £1 each and 8,280,000 ordinary shares of £1 each.

Required

Calculate the basic earnings per share (EPS) in respect of the year ended 31 December 20X4 on the basis that there was no change in the issued share capital of the company during the year ended 31 December 20X4.

Solution

$$\text{EPS} = \frac{£2{,}760{,}000 - £276{,}000 - £276{,}000}{8{,}280{,}000} = 26.7\text{p}$$

Issue of shares at full market price

In the example of Gerard plc, suppose that the company had issued 3,312,000 shares at full market value on 30 June 20X4. We would need to reflect this in the earnings per share working by recognising the impact on the earnings using a weighted average number of shares.

Date	*Actual number of shares*	*Fraction of year*	*Total*
1 January 20X4	8,280,000	$\frac{6}{12}$	4,140,000
30 June 20X4	11,592,000 (W1)	$\frac{6}{12}$	5,796,000
Number of shares in EPS calculation			9,936,000

(W1) New number of shares

Original number	8,280,000
New issue	3,312,000
New number	11,592,000

$$\text{Revised EPS} = \frac{£2{,}760{,}00 - £276{,}000 - £276{,}000}{9{,}936{,}000} = 22.2\text{p}$$

Bonus issue of shares

Suppose now that the company made no issue of shares at full price but instead made a bonus issue on 1 October 20X4 of one ordinary share for every four shares in issue at 30 September 20X4.

A bonus issue causes no impact on earnings, therefore EPS can simply be calculated based on the new number of shares.

8,280,000 × ¼ =	2,070,000 extra shares
Original number of shares	8,280,000
New number of shares	10,350,000

$$\text{Revised EPS} = \frac{£2{,}208{,}000}{10{,}350{,}000} = 21.3\text{p}$$

When a rights issue takes place

Suppose now that Gerard's only share issue in 20X4 was a rights issue of £1 ordinary shares on 1 October 20X4 in the proportion of one for every five shares held at a price of £1.20. The middle market price for the shares on the last day of quotation cum rights was £1.80 per share.

$$\text{Rights issue bonus fraction} = \frac{\text{Actual cum rights price}}{\text{Theoretical ex rights price}}$$

$$\text{Theoretical ex rights price} = \frac{(5 \times £1.80) + £1.20}{5+1} = \frac{£10.20}{6} = £1.70$$

$$\text{Therefore rights issue bonus fraction} = \frac{£1.80}{£1.70}$$

Date	*Actual number of shares*	*Fraction of year*	*Rights issue bonus fraction*	*Total*
1 Jan 20X4	8,280,000	$\frac{9}{12}$	$\frac{1.80}{1.70}$	6,575,294
1 Oct 20X4	9,936,000 (W1)	$\frac{3}{12}$		2,484,000
Number of shares to be used in EPS calculation				9,059,294

Revised EPS = $\frac{£2,208,000}{9,059,294}$ = 24.4p.

Workings

(W1) New number of shares

8,280,000 × 1 ÷ 5 = 1,656,000 extra shares

New number of shares = 8,280,000 + 1,656,000 = 9,936,000

CHAPTER 11

Tangible fixed assets

1 *FRS 15: Tangible fixed assets*

Definitions

- **Tangible fixed assets**

  Assets that have physical substance and are held for use in the production or supply of goods or services, for rental to others, or for administrative purposes on a continuing basis in the reporting entity's activities.

- **Depreciation**

  The measure of the cost or revalued amount of the economic benefits of the tangible fixed asset that have been consumed during the period.

  Consumption includes the wearing out, using up or other reduction in the useful economic life of a tangible fixed asset whether arising from use, effluxion of time or obsolescence through either changes in technology or changes in demand for the goods and services produced by the asset.

Initial measurement

Initial measurement of the asset (whether acquired or self-constructed) should be at its **cost**.

Cost should include all costs directly attributable to bringing the asset into working condition for its intended use. Cost can include finance costs.

Finance costs directly attributable to the construction of a tangible fixed asset may be capitalised as part of the cost of the asset. Such capitalisation is optional.

Subsequent expenditure

Subsequent expenditure should be capitalised if it enhances the economic benefits of the asset in excess of its previously assessed standard of performance. Otherwise, subsequent expenditure that helps to maintain the asset's standard of performance (eg routine repairs and maintenance) should be charged to the profit and loss account as it is incurred.

Valuation

Revaluation of tangible fixed assets is allowed if a policy of revaluation is adopted. Just as with the capitalisation of interest, revaluation is optional rather than mandatory.

Conditions:

- All assets of the same class must be revalued.
- Once revalued, the carrying amount in each balance sheet must be current value.

  This requirement is met for properties, according to FRS 15, by a full valuation every five years and an interim valuation in year 3. Interim valuations should be carried out in years 1, 2 and 4 if it is likely there has been a material change in value.

Reporting valuation gains and losses

- Gains

  Show in the statement of total recognised gains and losses (STRGL) unless they reverse previous losses recognised in the profit and loss account, when they can be taken to the profit and loss account.
- Losses
  - Losses caused by consumption of economic benefits – show in profit and loss account
  - Other losses – show in STRGL until the carrying amount reaches depreciated historical cost, then the excess balance thereafter in the profit and loss account.
- In reporting gains and losses, material revaluation gains and losses on individual assets in a class of assets should **not** be offset.

Gains and losses on disposal

Gains and losses on disposal of tangible fixed assets are shown in the profit and loss account and are calculated as the difference between proceeds and carrying amount. On disposal, the revaluation reserve of a revalued asset becomes a realised (distributable) reserve, but is not included in the reported profits for the period.

Depreciation

The depreciable amount (cost or valuation, less residual value) of a tangible fixed asset should be allocated on a systematic basis over its useful economic life. The depreciation method used should reflect as fairly as possible the pattern in which the asset's economic benefits are consumed. The entire depreciation charge on previously revalued assets must be charged to the profit and loss account.

FRS 15 mentions the straight-line method and the reducing balance method, but does not require any specific method. It is up to the directors to choose the method that most fairly reflects the asset's consumption pattern.

A change from one method of depreciation to another should only be made if the new method will give a fairer presentation of the results and financial position. Such a change does not constitute a change of accounting policy.

The carrying amount of the asset is depreciated using the revised method over the remaining useful life, beginning in the period in which the change is made.

Where the tangible fixed asset comprises two or more major components with different useful economic lives, each component should be accounted for separately for depreciation purposes and depreciated over its individual useful economic life.

There should be an **annual** review of the useful economic life and, if material, of the residual value of the assets. Any change should be reflected in future depreciation charges.

Disclosures

The following information should be disclosed separately in the financial statements for each class of tangible fixed assets:

- the depreciation methods used;
- the useful economic lives or the depreciation rates used;
- total depreciation charge for the period;
- where material, the financial effect of a change during the period in either the estimate of useful economic lives or the estimate of residual values;
- the cost or revalued amount at the beginning of the financial period and at the balance sheet date;
- the cumulative amount of provisions for depreciation or impairment at the beginning of the financial period and at the balance sheet date;
- a reconciliation of the movements, separately disclosing additions, disposals, revaluations, transfers, depreciation, impairment losses, and reversals of past impairment losses written back in the financial period;
- the net carrying amount at the beginning of the financial period and at the balance sheet date;
- where there has been a change in the depreciation method used, the effect, if material, should be disclosed in the period of change. The reason for the change should also be disclosed.

For each class of revalued assets, the following should be disclosed:

- the name and qualifications of the valuer or the valuer's organisation and a description of its nature;
- the basis or bases of valuation (including whether notional directly attributable acquisition costs have been included or expected selling costs deducted);

- the date and amounts of the valuations;
- where historical cost records are available, the carrying amount that would have been included in the financial statements had the tangible fixed assets been carried at historical cost less depreciation;
- whether the person(s) carrying out the valuation is (are) internal or external to the entity.

2 SSAP 19: Accounting for investment properties

Definition

An investment property is an interest in land and/or completed buildings which is held for its investment potential, any rental income being negotiated at arm's length.

Property owned by a company and occupied for its own purposes, or let to and occupied by another group company, is not an investment property.

Accounting treatment

Investment properties should not be depreciated. Instead, they are revalued annually at their open market value, gains and losses being taken to an investment revaluation reserve and included in the STRGL. If a deficit is expected to be permanent, it should be charged to the profit and loss account.

3 SSAP 4: Accounting for government grants

Definition

Government includes central, local and international government and their agencies.

Accounting treatment

Revenue grants (grants received to help pay for revenue expenditure)

Revenue grants are recognised in the period in which the related expenditure is recognised.

Capital grants (grants received to help pay for fixed assets)

SSAP 4 identifies two acceptable methods:

- Crediting the grant to the asset account concerned, leading to a reduction in annual depreciation charges, or
- Crediting the grant to a deferred income account, released to the credit of the profit and loss account in step with depreciation.

The adoption of the first method would contravene the Companies Act requirement that fixed assets should initially be stated at cost, so cannot be used by companies.

The second method is acceptable in all circumstances.

CHAPTER 12

Intangible fixed assets

1 FRS 10: Goodwill and intangible assets

Definitions

Purchased goodwill is the difference between the cost of an acquired entity and the aggregate of the fair values of that entity's identifiable assets and liabilities.

Non-purchased (or inherent) goodwill is any other goodwill.

Intangible assets are non-financial fixed assets that do not have physical substance but are identifiable and are controlled by the entity through custody or legal rights.

Accounting for goodwill

Inherent goodwill

Inherent goodwill should not be recognised in the balance sheet, due to the subjectivity required to value it. It should be ignored.

Positive purchased goodwill

Positive purchased goodwill should be recognised as an intangible fixed asset and amortised through the profit and loss account over its useful economic life.

There is a rebuttable presumption that the useful life does not exceed 20 years from the date of acquisition. However it is possible for goodwill to have a life greater than 20 years, or even an indefinite life.

If a useful life of more than 20 years is used, annual impairment reviews must be carried out on the goodwill balance (in accordance with FRS 11 – see later) to demonstrate the durability of the acquired business.

No residual value may be placed on goodwill in calculating the annual amortisation charge. The straight line method of amortisation should normally be used.

Negative purchased goodwill

If an acquisition appears to give rise to negative goodwill, first the fair values of the net assets acquired should be checked carefully to ensure that they have not been overstated. Negative goodwill remaining after this check should be recognised and separately disclosed on the face of the balance sheet, immediately below the goodwill heading. A subtotal should show the net total of positive and negative goodwill.

Negative goodwill up to the fair value of the non-monetary assets acquired should be recognised in the profit and loss account in the periods in which the non-monetary assets are recovered, whether through depreciation or sale.

Any negative goodwill in excess of the fair value of the non-monetary assets acquired should be recognised in the profit and loss account in the periods expected to benefit. It would be rare for any excess negative goodwill to arise in this way.

Accounting for other intangible assets

Internally generated intangible assets

Internally developed intangible assets should be capitalised only where they have a readily ascertainable market value.

Purchased intangible assets

An intangible asset purchased separately from a business should be capitalised at its cost.

An intangible asset acquired as part of the acquisition of a business should be capitalised separately from goodwill if its value can be measured reliably on initial recognition. Otherwise it should be subsumed into the amount of the purchase price paid for goodwill.

Once capitalised, the requirements for amortising intangible assets are the same as for goodwill.

2 SSAP 13: Accounting for research and development

Definitions

Pure (or basic) research: original investigation undertaken in order to gain new scientific or technical knowledge and understanding. Basic research is not primarily directed towards any specific practical aim or application.

Applied research: original investigation undertaken in order to gain new scientific or technical knowledge and directed towards a specific practical aim or objective.

Development: use of scientific or technical knowledge in order to produce new or substantially improved materials, devices, products, processes, systems or services prior to the commencement of commercial production.

Accounting treatment

Expenditure on pure and applied research (other than on fixed assets) should be written off through the profit and loss account in the year of expenditure.

In general, SSAP 13 requires that development expenditure should also be written off in the year of expenditure. However, it permits the deferral of such expenditure, to the extent that its recovery can reasonably be regarded as assured, if all the following circumstances apply.

- There is a clearly defined project.
- The related expenditure is separately identifiable.
- The outcome of such a project has been assessed with reasonable certainty as to:
  - its technical feasibility, and
  - its ultimate commercial viability.
- The aggregate of the deferred development costs, any further development costs, and related production, selling and administration costs is reasonably expected to be exceeded by related future sales or other revenues.
- Adequate resources exist, or are reasonably expected to be available, to enable the project to be completed and to provide any consequential increases in working capital.

Amortisation

Amortisation of deferred development costs should commence with the commercial production of the product or process, and should be allocated on a systematic basis to each accounting period over which the product or process is expected to be sold or used.

Deferred development expenditure should be reviewed at the end of each accounting period and written off to the extent that it is deemed irrecoverable.

Disclosure requirements of SSAP 13

(a) The accounting policy on R&D expenditure should be stated and explained.

(b) The total amount of R&D expenditure charged in the profit and loss account should be disclosed, analysed between the current year's expenditure and amounts amortised from deferred expenditure (see below).

(c) Movements on deferred development expenditure and the amount carried forward at the beginning and end of the period should be disclosed.

(d) Deferred development expenditure should be disclosed under intangible fixed assets in the balance sheet.

Note: The disclosure requirement (b) outlined above applies only to companies that are:

(1) (i) public limited companies; or
 (ii) special category companies (eg banks or insurance companies); or
 (iii) holding companies with a PLC or special category company as a subsidiary;

or

(2) exceed the criteria, multiplied by 10, for defining a medium-sized company (S248 CA 1985).

All the other requirements of SSAP 13 apply to all financial statements intended to give a true and fair view.

3 FRS 11: Impairment of fixed assets and goodwill

Definitions

Impairment has occurred when recoverable amount is less than carrying amount.

Recoverable amount is the higher of net realisable value and value in use.

Net realisable value is expected selling price, less any direct selling costs.

Value in use is the present value of the future cash flows arising from an asset.

Accounting issues

It is a long established principle that assets should not be included in the balance sheet at an amount greater than their recoverable amount (CA 85).

FRS 11 was issued to give guidance in the accounting for impairments.

The main requirements are as follows.

When an impairment test should be carried out

- Only necessary where there is an indication of impairment (eg a slump in the property market).
- In the absence of such indications it is assumed that there is no impairment.

Application of impairment test

- An asset is impaired when recoverable amount is less than carrying value.
- Therefore need to compare these two amounts and recognise an impairment loss if an impairment has occurred.

Treatment of impairment loss

If	*Recognise in*
Carrying value falls to an amount greater than depreciated historical cost	Statement of total recognised gains and losses
Carrying value falls to below depreciated historical cost	Statement of total recognised gains and losses (difference between carrying value and depreciated historical cost) Profit and loss account (amount below depreciated historical cost)

Income-generating units

Where possible, individual fixed assets should be tested for impairment. However, where cash flows cannot be identified as arising from individual assets, the impairment test should be carried out on the smallest group of assets (the income-generating unit) that produces an independent income stream.

CHAPTER 13

Stocks

1 Valuation of stocks

The amount at which stocks and work in progress is stated should be the total of the lower of *cost* and *net realisable value* of the *separate* items of stock and work in progress or of groups of similar items.

Cost is defined as being that expenditure which has been incurred in the normal course of business in bringing the product or service to its present location and condition.

Note that only costs incurred in the normal course of business should be included; thus if a lorry bringing items from France broke down, the costs of the break-down would not be included as part of the transport costs in the stock valuation since they are considered abnormal.

Cost includes cost of conversion, which comprises not only direct expenses of production but also production overheads based on the normal level of activity.

Net realisable value is defined as:

> 'the actual or estimated selling price (net of trade but before settlement discounts) less all further costs to completion and all costs to be incurred in marketing, selling and distributing the product'.

2 Methods of costing

Normally acceptable methods of determining cost:

- *Unit cost* – The actual cost of purchasing or manufacturing identifiable units of stock.
- *Weighted average cost* – The calculation of the cost of stocks and work in progress on the basis of the application to the units of stocks on hand of an average price computed by dividing the total cost of units by the total number of such units.
- *FIFO (first in, first out)* – The calculation of the cost of stocks and work in progress on the basis that the quantities in hand represent the latest purchases or production.
- *Standard cost* – The calculation of the cost of stocks and work in progress on the basis of periodically predetermined costs calculated from management's estimates of expected levels of costs, operations, operational efficiency, and the related expenditure. Standards must be reviewed frequently to ensure that they bear a reasonable relationship to the actual costs of the period.

- *Selling price less an estimated profit margin* – This is acceptable only if it can be clearly shown that it gives a reasonable approximation of the actual cost.

The following methods are normally not acceptable:

- *LIFO (last in, first out)* – The calculation of the cost of stocks and work in progress on the basis that the quantities in hand represent the earliest purchases or production.
- *Base stock* – The calculation of the cost of stocks and work in progress on the basis that a fixed unit value is ascribed to a predetermined number of units of stock, any excess over this number being valued on the basis of some other method. If the number of units in stock is less than the predetermined minimum, the fixed unit value is applied to the number in stock.

Example

RJ plc made the following purchases and sales of grommets in May 20X1:

1 May	Opening stock	Nil
8 May	Bought 200 units	@ £5 each
13 May	Bought 400 units	@ £5.60 each
20 May	Sold 300 units	@ £8 each

Determine the closing stock valuation at 31 May and the gross profit for the month using:

(a) FIFO

(b) LIFO

(c) Weighted average cost

Solution

(a)	Closing stock	=	300 units @ £5.60	=	£1,680
	Gross profit	=	£2,400 – (200 × £5 + 100 × £5.60)	=	£840
(b)	Closing stock	=	(200 × £5 + 100 × £5.60)	=	£1,560
	Gross profit	=	£2,400 – (300 × £5.60)	=	£720
(c)	Average price	=	$\frac{200 \times £5 + 400 \times £5.60}{600 \text{units}}$	=	£5.40
	Therefore closing stock	=	300 × £5.40	=	£1,620
	Gross profit	=	£2,400 – (300 × £5.40)	=	£780

CHAPTER 14

Tax in company accounts

1 FRS 16: Current tax

Dividends receivable and payable should be shown in the profit and loss account **excluding** attributable tax credits.

A *withholding tax* is tax on dividends or other income that is deducted by the payer of the income and paid to the tax authorities wholly on behalf of the recipient.

FRS 16 states that all interest and other amounts payable or receivable should be shown *including* withholding taxes.

Disclosure summary

Profit and loss account

	£
Income	
Dividends received from UK companies (net, ie not grossed up for tax credits)	X
Interest and royalties received (gross up for income tax deducted)	X
Expenditure	
Debenture interest paid (gross up for income tax deducted)	X
Tax on profits on ordinary activities (Note)	X

Note: Tax on profits on ordinary activities

Corporation tax on profits on ordinary activities @ x%	X
Under/(over) provision in previous year	X/(X)
Tax charge for the year	X

Balance sheet (extract)

	£
Creditors: amounts falling due within one year	
Proposed dividend (not grossed up for tax credits)	X
Other creditors including taxation and social security	
Income tax due to Revenue (difference between IT deducted from debenture interest paid and IT suffered on royalty income)	X
Corporation tax payable (this year's CT charge)	X

2 Deferred tax

Accounting profits and taxable profits

The amount of current taxation payable on the profits of a particular period may bear little relationship to the reported profit before tax appearing in the published accounts. The difference comes from two sources: permanent differences and timing differences.

Permanent differences arise where items taken into account for the purpose of the financial accounts are disallowable or non-taxable for tax purposes. An example might be disallowable entertaining expenses. This is a permanent difference because no tax relief will ever be received for such expenditure, even though it is quite properly deducted as an expense when computing accounting profits.

Timing differences arise when certain types of income and expenditure are recognised in different periods for the purpose of financial accounts on the one hand and taxation on the other, eg capital allowances.

Deferred taxation is a system of dealing with the distortions caused by timing differences. It is not concerned at all with permanent differences. The objective of deferred taxation is to ensure that the tax charge shown in the profit and loss account is not out of line with the amount of profit earned.

3 Bases for providing for deferred tax

Three possible approaches have been suggested to deal with the problem of timing differences: nil provision, partial provision and full provision.

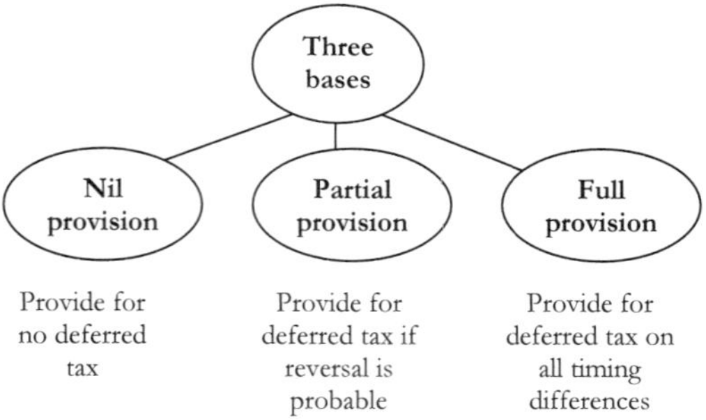

Example

Peter Ltd was incorporated on 1 April 20X1. In the year ended 31 March 20X2 the company made a profit before tax of £100,000 (after charging depreciation of £10,000) and purchased plant for £48,000 and motor vehicles for £12,000.

Corporation tax is chargeable at the rate of 30%, and writing down allowances are available at 25%.

Compute the following:

(a) The corporation tax payable for the year ended 31 March 20X2.

(b) The deferred tax charge for the year on the basis that full provision is made for all originating timing differences, showing also the relevant extracts from the financial statements.

Solution

(a)

	£
Reported profit	100,000
Add back depreciation	10,000
	110,000
Less: Capital allowance (48,000 + 12,000) × 25%	(15,000)
Taxable profit	95,000

Tax payable is therefore £95,000 × 30% = £28,500.

(b) Identify the timing difference by comparing accumulated depreciation to cumulative capital allowances.

	£
Depreciation	10,000
Capital allowance	(15,000)
Originating timing difference	(5,000)

Tax deferred is therefore £5,000 × 30% = £1,500.

You will then need to make a provision for deferred tax.

Debit Taxation charge (profit and loss)

Credit Provision for deferred tax (shown in the balance sheet under 'Provisions for liabilities and charges')

This leads to the following extracts from the accounts.

Extract from balance sheet at 31 March 20X2

	£
Provisions for liabilities and charges	
Deferred tax	1,500

Extract from profit and loss account for the year ended 31 March 20X2

	£	£
Profit before tax		100,000
Taxation		
UK corporation tax at 30%	28,500	
Deferred tax	1,500	
		30,000
Profit after tax		70,000

4 *FRS 19: Deferred tax*

In December 2000 the ASB brought the UK into line with international practice by issuing FRS 19 which requires the full provision basis for calculating deferred tax.

The requirements of FRS 19

Deferred tax must be recognised in full on the following sorts of timing differences:

- accelerated capital allowances (as seen earlier, where the capital allowances granted against taxable profits exceed the depreciation charge made against accounting profits);
- accruals for pension costs that will be deductible for tax purposes only when paid;
- elimination of unrealised intra-group profits on consolidation;
- unrelieved tax losses;
- other short-term timing differences (those that originate in one period and are expected to reverse in the following period).

Deferred tax should not be recognised when:

- a fixed asset is revalued without there being any commitment to sell the asset; or
- the gain on sale of an asset is rolled over into replacement assets.

5 *SSAP 5: Accounting for VAT*

- *Turnover* – Turnover shown in the profit and loss account should exclude VAT on taxable outputs.
- *Irrecoverable VAT* – Irrecoverable VAT relating to fixed assets and to other items disclosed separately in published accounts should be included in their cost where practicable and material.

CHAPTER 15

Leases

1 Types of extended credit agreement

Credit sale – involves a contract of sale with payment by instalments. Ownership of the goods passes on delivery by the supplier, and a binding debt is created which cannot be avoided by returning the goods.

Hire purchase – goods are supplied on hire to customers until, on fulfillment of certain conditions (usually the payment of an agreed number of instalments), the customer becomes entitled to purchase the asset (usually for a nominal amount). Legal title passes to the customer at this point.

Lease – involves a contract under which the lessor hires an asset to the lessee. The lessor will always retain ownership of the asset but conveys the right to use the asset to the lessee for an agreed period of time, in return for the payment of specific rentals.

SSAP 21 definitions

A *finance lease* is a lease that transfers substantially all the risks and rewards of ownership of an asset to the lessee. It should be presumed that such a transfer of risks and rewards occurs if at the inception of a lease the present value of the minimum lease payments, including any initial payment, amounts to substantially all (normally 90% or more) of the fair value of the leased asset. The present value should be calculated by using the interest rate implicit in the lease. If the fair value of the asset is not determinable, an estimate thereof should be used.

An *operating lease* is a lease other than a finance lease.

The *minimum lease payments* are the minimum payments that the lessee has contracted to pay the lessor under the terms of the lease.

Accounting treatment

SSAP 21 *Accounting for Leases and Hire Purchase Contracts* requires that finance leases (or equivalent agreements) are capitalised in the lessee's balance sheet by including both:

- the value of the asset in fixed assets; and
- the outstanding lease commitment in creditors.

The profit and loss account is charged with depreciation on the asset and an appropriate share of the finance charge each year.

The lessor will account for future amounts receivable under finance leases as a debtor, with the finance income allocated to the profit and loss account over the term of the lease.

For an operating lease it is the lessor that records the asset as a fixed asset and depreciates it. Rental is recognised on a straight-line basis in both the lessee's and the lessor's books over the lease term.

2 Accounting for finance leases

Three different methods are possible for calculating the interest included in each instalment.

- The straight line method (spreading the interest equally over the life of the asset – an unscientific method).
- The actuarial method (the most accurate method, reflecting the true interest arising in each period).
- The sum of the digits method (an approximation to the actuarial method).

Example

On 1 January 20X1 a company acquires the use of an asset which has a fair value of £10,000 on a lease, the terms of which are that they pay a deposit of £575 followed by seven annual instalments of £2,000 payable in arrears. The interest rate implicit in the lease is 11.4%.

	£
Fair value (cash)	10,000
Amounts paid under terms of lease	
Deposit	(575)
Instalments (7 × £2,000)	(14,000)
Total interest	4,575

We will write up the obligations under finance leases account for the first two years.

Obligations under finance leases

	£		£
Year 1			
Cash deposit	575	Fair value	10,000
Cash instalment	2,000	Interest ((10,000 – 575) × 11.4%)	1,074
Balance c/d	8,499		
	11,074		11,074

Year 2

Cash instalment	2,000	Balance b/d	8,499
Balance c/d	7,468	Interest (8,499 × 11.4%)	969
	9,468		9,468
		Balance b/d	7,468

In year 1 the profit and loss account will be charged with interest of £1,074.

There will also be depreciation charge for the asset, which if it is to be straight line depreciation will be £1,429.

In the balance sheet at the end of year 1, the obligation under finance leases would be shown as follows:

	£
Creditors: amounts falling due within one year	
Obligations under finance leases (8,499 – 7,468)	1,031
Creditors: amounts falling due after more than one year	
Obligations under finance leases	7,468

3 Operating leases

Accounting treatment

- The rental under an operating lease should be charged on a straight-line basis over the lease term.
- The asset should not be capitalised.

4 Disclosure requirements of SSAP 21

Disclosure requirements by lessees

Typical disclosure would be as follows (using the figures from the previous example at the end of year 1).

- **Assets held under finance leases**

  The net book value of fixed assets of £X includes an amount of £8,571 in respect of assets held under finance leases.

- **Obligations under finance leases**

  The minimum lease payments to which the company is committed fall due as follows:

	£	£
Within one year		2,000
Over one year		
In the 2nd to 5th years inclusive	8,000	
Over 5 years	2,000	
		10,000
		12,000
Amount representing future financing charges (4,575 - 1,074)		3,501
Obligations under finance leases		8,499

The other required disclosures are illustrated below:

- **Profit is stated after charging:**

	£
Depreciation of owned assets	X
Depreciation of assets held under finance leases and hire purchase contracts	1,429
Interest payable – bank loans and overdrafts	X
Finance charges payable – finance leases and hire purchase contracts	1,074
Hire of plant and machinery – operating leases	X
Hire of other assets – operating leases	X

- **Operating lease commitments**

  At 31 December 20X7 the company had annual commitments under non-cancellable operating leases as set out below.

	20X7		*20X6*	
	Land and buildings	*Other*	*Land and buildings*	*Other*
	£000	£000	£000	£000
Operating leases which expire				
within one year	X	X	X	X
in the second to fifth years inclusive	X	X	X	X
over five years	X	X	X	X
	X	X	X	X

CHAPTER 16

Post balance sheet events and contingencies

1 *SSAP 17: Accounting for post balance sheet events*

Key definitions

- Post balance sheet events: events occurring between the balance sheet date and the date on which the board approves the financial statements.
- Adjusting events: post balance sheet events which provide additional evidence of conditions existing at the year end.
- Non–adjusting events: post balance sheet events concerning conditions not existing at the year end.

Accounting treatment

Prepare financial statements on the basis of conditions existing at the balance sheet date.

Adjust financial statements where:

- a material adjusting event occurs; or
- there is an indication that the going concern concept is no longer appropriate.

Disclose in financial statements:

- material non-adjusting events; or
- 'window dressing' of the accounts.

2 *FRS 12: Provisions, contingent liabilities and contingent assets*

FRS 12 attempts to prevent the manipulation of profits.

The objective of the standard in relation to provisions is to ensure that:

- provisions are recognised and measured consistently;
- sufficient information is disclosed to enable a user of the accounts to understand the nature, timing and amount of any provisions included in the accounts.

Recognition of a provision

A provision is defined as a liability where there is uncertainty over either the timing or the amount of the future expenditure.

A provision should only be recognised when:

- the entity has a legal or constructive obligation as a result of past events;
- it is probable that a transfer of economic benefits will be required to settle the obligation; and
- a reliable estimate can be made of the amount needed to settle the obligation.

Detailed guidance is given on the following specific situations.

- Future operating losses – no provisions should be recognised for such losses, but the assets relating to the loss-making operation may need to be reviewed for impairment.
- Reorganisation costs – provision should only be made where the entity is demonstrably committed to the reorganisation.
- Onerous contracts – these are contracts where the unavoidable costs of meeting the terms of the contract exceed the expected revenues (for instance, where an entity is committed to continuing the lease on a vacant property); provision should be made for the net loss that is expected to arise.
- Environmental liabilities – provision should be made when the entity becomes legally or constructively obliged to rectify the damage it has caused, but the creation of environmental contamination does not in itself give rise to such an obligation.
- Major refurbishment programmes – a business may have to undertake a major refurbishment programme every few years in order to continue its operations, but it does not have an obligation to transfer economic benefits until each refurbishment has been completed and the related payment is due. It is therefore not acceptable to recognise a provision for such costs in the years between actual refurbishments.

Measurement of a provision

The amount recognised as a provision should be the best estimate of the expenditure needed to settle the obligation existing at the balance sheet date, and provisions should be discounted whenever the effect of this is material.

Disclosure of provisions

- A brief description of the nature of the obligation and the timing of the payment.
- The amount provided and the basis of any estimates.
- Details of movements during the year, showing separately additions and adjustments, amounts used in the year, amounts released unused, the amortisation of any discount and the effect of any exchange differences.
- Where relevant, the discount rate used.

Accounting for contingencies

The objective of FRS 12 in relation to contingencies is to ensure that:

- contingencies are recognised and measured consistently;
- sufficient information is disclosed to enable a user of the accounts to understand the nature, amount and uncertainties relating to any contingencies.

Definition of a contingent liability/asset: a possible obligation/asset that arises from past events and whose existence will be confirmed only by the occurrence of uncertain future events not wholly within the entity's control.

Contingent liabilities also include obligations that are not recognised because:

- it is not probable that a transfer of economic benefits will be required; or
- the amount of the obligation cannot be measured reliably.

Contingent liabilities should not be recognised. They should be disclosed unless they are remote.

Contingent assets should not be recognised. They should be disclosed where they are probable.

CHAPTER 17

Other accounting standards

1 *FRS 4: Capital instruments*

All that is required for Unit 11 is the definition of capital instruments.

Definition

The FRS 4 definition of a capital instrument is as follows:

> 'All instruments that are issued by reporting entities as a means of raising finance, including shares, debentures, loans and debt instruments, options and warrants that give the holder the right to subscribe for or obtain capital instruments'.

2 *FRS 5: Reporting the substance of transactions*

Objective of FRS 5

The objective of FRS 5 is to ensure that the substance of an entity's transactions is reported in its financial statements.

Types of transactions

For the vast majority of transactions their commercial substance and their legal form will be one and the same thing. However, the FRS indicates three general types of transactions where care should be taken that the true commercial substance is recognised where:

- the person benefiting from an asset is not the legal owner;
- the transaction is linked to others in such a way that the true commercial effect can only be understood by considering the whole series of transactions;
- an option is included in the transaction where its terms make it highly likely that it will be exercised.

Recognition of assets and liabilities

The key to determining the substance of a transaction is to identify whether it has given rise to new assets or liabilities or increased or decreased the existing assets and liabilities.

3 FRS 8: Related party disclosures

Definitions

(a) Two or more parties are **related parties** if:

- (i) one party controls the other party; or
- (ii) the parties are subject to common control from the same source; or
- (iii) one party has significant influence over the other party; or
- (iv) the parties are subject to significant influence from the same source.

(b) A **related party transaction** is the transfer of assets or liabilities or the performance of services by, to or for a related party irrespective of whether a price is charged.

Examples of related parties

The following are related parties:

(a) companies in the same group (eg holding company and subsidiary).

(b) associates and joint ventures of the reporting entity (where the reporting entity has influence but not control over an investment, for example the reporting company might own 40% of the shares of another company).

(c) directors of the reporting entity.

(d) pension funds for the benefit of employees of the reporting entity.

The following are assumed to be related parties unless the contrary can be demonstrated:

(a) the key management of the reporting entity (those in senior positions, even if they are not directors).

(b) a person owning more than 20% of the voting rights of the reporting entity.

(c) persons acting together in such a way as to be able to control or significantly influence the reporting entity.

(d) an entity managing or managed by the reporting entity under a management contract.

If an individual is a related party of the reporting entity, then all members of his close family are also presumed to be related parties.

Disclosures required of related party transactions

FRS 8 states that material transactions with a related party must be disclosed.

4 FRS 17: Retirement benefits

Types of pension scheme

There are two sorts of pension scheme available:

(a) In a **defined contribution scheme**, an employer pays into the scheme regular contributions which are fixed as an amount or as a percentage of pay. On retirement, the size of the member's benefits depends on the size of the fund which has accumulated to that date. This will depend on the size of the amounts paid in, and the investment returns achieved by the scheme managers.

(b) In a **defined benefit scheme**, the scheme rules define the benefits payable, independently of the contributions paid in. The size of the benefits payable is not directly related to the investment performance of the scheme assets.

5 Accounting for defined contribution schemes

Accounting for a defined contribution scheme is simple, since the employer company has no further liability after paying the agreed contributions payable to the scheme.

The pension cost for a period is equal to the contributions payable to the scheme for the period.

A prepayment or accrual might arise if the employer company has made too large or too small a payment to the scheme. These will be shown in current assets or current liabilities in the normal way.

6 Accounting for defined benefit schemes

This is more complicated, since estimates of the future will be required, concerning future investment returns, future salary increases, deaths before retirement etc. The professional advice of an actuary is required to advise on such matters. The actuary will recommend a contribution rate to be applied now to build up sufficient assets to meet the future liabilities of the scheme.

Measuring the assets of defined benefit schemes

Defined benefit scheme assets should be measured at fair value, so that:

- quoted securities should be at mid-market value;
- unquoted securities should be at estimated fair value;
- property should be at open market value.

Measuring the liabilities of defined benefit schemes

The scheme liabilities comprise the benefits promised under the formal terms of the scheme, plus any constructive obligations for further benefits that the employer cannot avoid.

The scheme liabilities should be measured using an actuarial basis, ie estimating the future cash flows arising under the actuarial assumptions and then discounting these cash flows at an appropriate discount rate.

Accounting for the surplus or deficit

The excess/shortfall in the value of the assets over the present value of the liabilities is the actuarial surplus/deficit in the scheme. The employer and actuary will consult on whether and how to clear the surplus or deficit.

The employer should recognise a surplus as an asset in his balance sheet to the extent that he will benefit from reduced contributions in the future or refunds from the scheme.

The employer should recognise a deficit as a liability in his balance sheet to the extent that it reflects a legal or constructive obligation.

The asset or liability arising should be shown on the face of the balance sheet separately from any sundry prepayments or accruals arising from the timing of the payments of contributions to the scheme.

7 SSAP 20: Foreign currency translation

A business can have dealings in foreign currencies in one of two ways:

- by directly buying or selling goods in a foreign currency;
- by investing in a foreign subsidiary company.

Individual company transactions

When the transaction takes place the foreign currency amount will normally be translated at the actual rate of exchange on the date of the transaction. When the amount is paid or received, if the exchange rate has changed, then this will give rise to an exchange gain or loss.

A further problem arises if the goods have not been paid for by the end of the accounting period as there will be a debtor or creditor in the balance sheet for the amount due. According to SSAP 20 this should be translated at the exchange rate on the balance sheet date in order to give the fairest estimate of the actual amount due. This again may give rise to an exchange gain or loss.

These exchange gains or losses should be recognised in the profit and loss account for the year.

Foreign subsidiary companies

If a company buys a foreign subsidiary then at the year end the subsidiary's financial statements must be consolidated with those of the parent company. However, the subsidiary's own individual financial statements will be expressed in its own currency.

Therefore, before consolidation takes place, the subsidiary's financial statements must be translated into sterling. SSAP 20 lays down distinct rules as to how this translation is to be carried out.

8 Financial Reporting Standard for Smaller Entities

The FRSSE is aimed at the financial statements of companies that fall within the Companies Act definition of small companies.

Objective

The objective of the FRSSE is to ensure that these small companies provide in their financial statements information that is useful to the users of those statements in assessing the stewardship of management and for making economic decisions. The FRSSE recognises that the needs of users in small companies are different from those of users in other entities.

Content

The FRSSE is a summary of all of the measurement and disclosure requirements that a small company must follow when preparing their financial statements. It contains, in simplified form, the requirements from existing accounting standards that are relevant to these smaller entities. Therefore if a company complies with the FRSSE then they are exempt from the requirements of all other accounting standards.

CHAPTER 18

Interpretation of accounts

1 *Profitability ratios*

Return on capital employed (ROCE)

Capital employed is normally measured as fixed assets plus current assets less current liabilities, and represents the long-term investment in the business, or owners' capital plus long-term liabilities. Return on capital employed is frequently regarded as the best measure of profitability.

$$\text{ROCE} = \frac{\text{Profit before interest and taxation (PBIT)}}{\text{Capital employed}} \times 100\%$$

Note that the profit *before* interest is used, because the loan capital rewarded by that interest is included in capital employed.

A low return on capital employed (assets used) is caused by either a low profit margin or a low asset turnover or both. This can be seen by breaking down the primary ROCE ratio into its two components: profit margin and asset turnover.

$$\text{ROCE} = \frac{\text{PBIT}}{\text{Capital employed}}$$

$$= \text{Profit margin} \times \text{Asset turnover}$$

$$= \frac{\text{PBIT}}{\text{Sales}} \times \frac{\text{Sales}}{\text{Capital employed}}$$

Profit margin (on sales)

$$\text{Margin} = \frac{\text{Profit before interest and taxation}}{\text{Sales}} \times 100\%$$

A low margin indicates low selling prices or high costs or both.

Asset turnover

This will show how fully a company is utilising its assets.

$$\text{Asset turnover} = \frac{\text{Sales}}{\text{Capital employed}}$$

A low turnover shows that a company is not generating a sufficient volume of business for the size of the asset base. This may be remedied by increasing sales or by disposing of some of the assets or both.

Gross profit margin

$$\text{Margin} = \frac{\text{Gross profit}}{\text{Sales}} \times 100\%$$

The gross profit margin focuses on the trading account. A low margin could indicate selling prices too low or cost of sales too high.

Return on owners' equity

$$\text{Return} = \frac{\text{Profit after interest and preference dividends but before tax}}{\text{Ordinary share capital and reserves}} \times 100\%$$

This looks at the return earned for ordinary shareholders. We use the profit after preference dividends and interest (ie the amounts that have to be paid before ordinary shareholders can be rewarded).

2 *Liquidity ratios and asset utilisation*

Current ratio

This indicates the extent to which the claims of short–term creditors are covered by assets that are expected to be converted to cash.

$$\text{Current ratio} = \frac{\text{Current assets}}{\text{Current liabilities}}$$

Acid test ratio (quick ratio)

This is calculated in the same way as the current ratio except that stocks are excluded from current assets due to their relative lack of liquidity.

$$\text{Acid test ratio} = \frac{\text{Current assets - Stock}}{\text{Current liabilities}}$$

This ratio is a much better test of immediate solvency.

Debtors ratio

This is computed by dividing the debtors by the average daily sales to determine the number of days sales held in debtors.

$$\text{Average collection period} = \frac{\text{Trade debtors}}{\text{Credit sales}} \times 365 \text{ days}$$

A long average collection period probably indicates poor credit control.

Creditors ratio

This is computed by dividing the creditors by the average daily credit purchases to determine the number of days purchases held in creditors.

$$\text{Average payment period} = \frac{\text{Trade creditors}}{\text{Credit purchases}} \times 365 \text{ days}$$

Stock turnover

This ratio indicates whether stock levels are justified in relation to cost of sales. The higher the ratio, the healthier the cash flow position.

$$\text{Stock turnover} = \frac{\text{Cost of sales}}{\text{Stocks}}$$

Stock turnover can also be calculated in days as:

$$\text{Stockholding period} = \frac{\text{Stock}}{\text{Cost of sales}} \times 365 \text{ days}$$

3 *Investor ratios*

Earnings per share

$$\text{Earnings per share} = \frac{\text{Earnings available for ordinary shareholders}}{\text{Number of ordinary shares in issue}}$$

'Earnings available for ordinary shareholders' means profits after interest, taxation and preference dividends.

Earnings per share is used by investors in calculating the price earnings ratio or PE ratio. This is simply calculated as follows.

Price earnings ratio

$$\text{PE ratio} = \frac{\text{Market price of share}}{\text{Earnings per share}}$$

A high PE ratio means that the shares are seen as an attractive investment. For example, if the PE ratio is 20, it means that investors are prepared to pay 20 times the annual level of earnings in order to acquire the shares.

Dividend cover

$$\text{Dividend cover} = \frac{\text{Profit available to ordinary shareholders}}{\text{Dividend}}$$

This gives an indication of the security of future dividends. A high dividend cover ratio means that available profits comfortably cover the amount being paid out in dividends.

4 *Risk*

Gearing

Gearing measures the extent to which a business is dependent on borrowed funds, as opposed to equity funding.

Gearing gives an indication of long-term liquidity and the risk inherent within the business. Highly geared companies have to meet interest commitments before paying dividends and may have problems raising further finance if expansion is necessary.

Gearing

$$= \frac{\text{Long - term debt and preference share capital}}{\text{Shareholder funds and long - term debt and preference share capital}} \times 100\%$$

Interest cover

$$\text{Interest cover} = \frac{\text{Profit before interest}}{\text{Interest paid}}$$

Interest on debt has to be paid before shareholders can receive dividends. Therefore a good measure of risk is to compare available profit with the amount of interest to be paid.

Example

Now calculate all of the above ratios on the following profit and loss account and balance sheet for a company called J G Ltd.

Summarised balance sheet at 31 December 20X8

	£000	£000
Fixed assets		2,600
Current assets		
Stocks	600	
Debtors	900	
Balance at bank	100	
	1,600	
Trade creditors	800	
		800
		3,400
Debenture stock		1,400
		2,000
Capital and reserves		
Ordinary share capital (£1 shares)		1,000
Preference share capital		200
Profit and loss account		800
		2,000

Summarised profit and loss account for the year ended 31 December 20X8

	£000
Sales	6,000
Cost of sales (including purchases £4,300)	4,500
Gross profit	1,500
Administrative and distribution costs	1,160
Trading profit	340
Debenture interest	74
Profit before tax	266
Taxation	106
Profit after tax	160
Preference dividend	10
Profit available for ordinary shareholders	150
Ordinary dividend	10
Retained profit	140

Solution

ROCE	=	10%	340/3,400 × 100%
Profit margin	=	5.7%	340/6,000 × 100%
Asset turnover	=	1.8 times	6,000/3,400
Gross profit margin	=	25%	1,500/6,000 × 100%
Return on owners' equity	=	14.2%	(266 – 10)/(1,000 + 800) × 100%
Current ratio	=	2 times	1,600/800
Acid test ratio	=	1.25 times	(900 + 100)/800
Debtors ratio	=	55 days	900/6,000 × 365 days
Creditors ratio	=	68 days	800/4,300 × 365 days
Stock turnover	=	7.5 times	4,500/600
Stock turnover in days	=	49 days	600/4,500 × 365 days
Earnings per share	=	15p	150/1,000
Dividend cover	=	15 times	150/10
Gearing	=	47%	(1,400 + 200)/3,400 × 100%
Interest cover	=	4.6 times	340/74

Interpretation

The first stage of answering questions on interpretation is to calculate the ratios; the second is to draw conclusions about the company based on those ratios. A study of the trend of ratios for several years is desirable before drawing firm conclusions about many aspects of a company's position.

Let us consider what conclusions we may draw from the illustrative accounts of J G Ltd above.

Profitability

Return on capital employed – The company shows a return on total capital employed of 10%: not dramatically good, but satisfactory. Note that it exceeds the rate of interest being paid on the debentures (5.3%).

Net profit as percentage of sales – This is fairly low at 5.7%. The net profit as a percentage of sales varies greatly from industry to industry: more information is needed about the performance of other companies to draw useful conclusions about the level of this ratio.

Asset turnover ratio – The overall efficiency may be judged by asset turnover. This is 1.8 times for J G Ltd.

Gross profit margin – This is a more respectable 25% but again comparison to the industry average would indicate whether it is acceptable.

Return on owners' equity – The level of acceptability of 14.2% will depend on three things.

- The investors' anticipated return.
- The industry average or that of competitors.
- The return available in other forms of investment, eg building society.

Liquidity

A quick ratio of about 1:1 is normally regarded as indicating a reasonable level of liquidity. The current ratio is often more variable, because of variations in a company's need to hold stocks.

We may deduce either that the nature of J G Ltd's business is such that above–average stock levels are needed, or that its stock control procedures leave something to be desired. More information is clearly needed. The stock turnover ratio may throw more light on this aspect: see 'asset utilisation' below.

Asset utilisation

Several ratios give some idea of management efficiency.

Asset turnover ratio – Unfortunately we can draw no conclusions whatsoever about the company and the efficiency of its management without more information to compare it with the ratios for J G Ltd in past years and the ratios for other similar companies in the current year.

Debtors ratio – J G Ltd's figure of 55 days is probably acceptable, since 60 days is often regarded as 'par' for a company offering normal credit terms of monthly settlement for all its sales.

Creditors ratio – J G Ltd is paying its creditors on average in 68 days. This is after the period from which it collects its debtors (55 days) so it will help cash flow overall.

Stock turnover ratio – This comes to 7.5 times or 49 days for J G Ltd. It is again difficult to draw conclusions about this figure in isolation. It needs to be compared with other years for J G Ltd and with other companies.

Investor ratios

Earnings per share – J G Ltd's earnings per share is 15p. This should be compared to J G Ltd's earnings per share achieved in prior years to determine whether the trend is favourable or not.

Dividend cover – This is fifteen times, a very secure profit to dividend ratio.

Risk

The gearing ratio for J G Ltd is 47%. Anything over 50% would probably be regarded as fairly high.

Interest cover – For J G Ltd this is 4.6 times. This may be considered reasonable.

5 General points about financial ratios

There are some more points on ratio analysis which should be particularly noted.

Caution in interpretation

Dogmatic conclusions should be avoided. Ratios rarely answer questions but they can highlight areas where questions might usefully be asked.

Balance sheet figures

Many of the ratios considered in this chapter involve the use of balance sheet figures. These ratios should be interpreted with caution since the balance sheet shows the position at a specific moment only and this may not be typical of the general position. This point is particularly important where the ratio is derived from a balance sheet figure in conjunction with a figure from the trading or profit and loss account. This is because the first figure relates to a moment in time whereas the second is a total for a period.

Other financial ratios

There are an almost infinite number of ratios which can be calculated from a set of final accounts. The ones shown above are those most commonly used in practice and include those which have been specifically asked about in assessments. It should be noted, however, that there are many other ratios which could be useful in particular contexts.

Partial sightedness of ratios

It is usually unwise to limit analysis and interpretation only to information revealed by ratios. There is the danger that excessive reliance on ratios in interpretation and analysis can lead to a 'blinkered' approach.

6 The working capital cycle

The working capital cycle

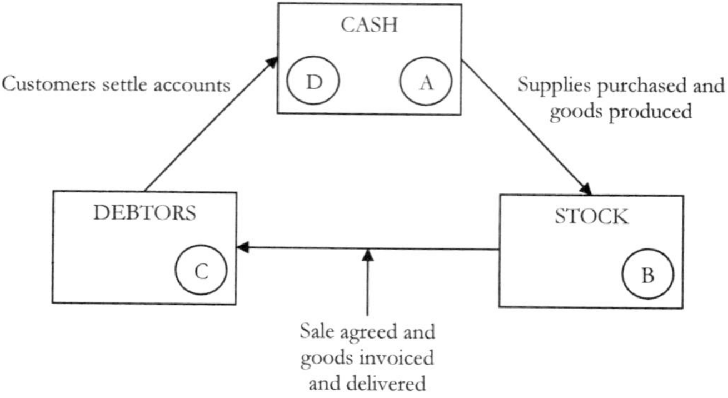

Effect on cash flows

All of these activities affect cash flows:

- acquisition of stock on credit helps cash flow temporarily;
- when creditors are paid cash flows out;
- while stocks are held, and until customers settle, cash is 'tied up', ie cash inflow is deferred;
- when customers settle, cash flows in.

Working capital management

The company must therefore ensure that stock levels are watched very carefully and that debtors' cash is collected on a timely basis whilst simultaneously monitoring the cash balance to ensure that sufficient funds are held for short-term requirements. Any genuinely surplus funds in excess of a working cash balance should be reinvested in higher interest accounts.

Pocket Notes Review Form

AAT UNIT 11 POCKET NOTES
DRAFTING FINANCIAL STATEMENTS

Thank you for choosing these FTC Foulks Lynch Pocket Notes for your AAT qualification. As we are constantly striving to improve our products, we would be grateful if you could provide us with feedback about how useful you found this publication.

Name:..

Address:..

....

Email:..

Overall opinion of these Pocket Notes

	Excellent	*Adequate*	*Poor*
Depth of technical coverage	☐	☐	☐
Clarity of explanations	☐	☐	☐
Clarity of definitions	☐	☐	☐
Diagrams	☐	☐	☐
Level of accuracy	☐	☐	☐
Size of book	☐	☐	☐
Layout/font used	☐	☐	☐
Index	☐	☐	☐

Did you spot any errors or ambiguities? Please let us have the details below.

Page	**Error**

Thank you for your feedback.

Please return this form to: Veronica Wastell, Publisher, FTC Foulks Lynch, FREEPOST NAT 17540, Wokingham RG40 1BR